A PICTORIAL ENCYCLOPEDIA
OF
DECORATIVE IRONWORK

Twelfth through Eighteenth Centuries

Edited and with an Historical Introduction by
Otto Hoever

DOVER PUBLICATIONS, INC.
Mineola, New York

Bibliographical Note

This Dover edition, first published in 2001, is an unabridged republication of the book originally published in 1927 by Ernest Benn Limited, London, under the title *An Encyclopedia of Ironwork*.

DOVER *Pictorial Archive* SERIES

Library of Congress Cataloging-in-Publication Data

A pictorial encyclopedia of decorative ironwork. Twelfth through eighteenth centuries / edited and with an historical introduction by Otto Hoever.
      p. cm.
  Originally published in 1927 by Ernest Benn, London, under the title An encyclopedia of ironwork.
  ISBN 0-486-41728-X (pbk.)
    1. Ironwork. 2. Decoration and ornament, Architectural. 3. Architecture—Details. I. Hoever, Otto.
NK8205 .P53 2001
739.4—dc21

                                          00-052305

Manufactured in the United States of America
Dover Publications, Inc., 31 East 2nd Street, Mineola, N.Y. 11501

CONTENTS

INTRODUCTION

Ornamental Ironwork

Although the most conspicuous productions of smithcraft are rarely the outcome of the ironworkers' own designs, nevertheless, ironwork translates into material many artistic conceptions, and reflects the art of various style-epochs, and countries.

It is a well-known fact that the iron bar is the base of all lineal ornamental ironwork, however manifold the various patterns may be. A number of bars can be arranged to make a trellis, or they may be made to serve as bindings and hinges, etc. The trellis, using the term in its widest sense, was the main object of technical and artistic treatment by the masters of smithcraft. The iron bars, fixed by rivets to the doors to protect them, constitute a complete lattice-work. We may say that the use of one of the three main classes of bars: flat, round, and square is a characteristic feature of a particular style. Thus, Early Gothic favoured either narrow or broad iron bands, and Late Gothic, in the north, the round bar. In the south, above all in Italy, the Renaissance introduces the square bar, which was also preferred by Rococo smiths, particularly by the French. It was during these periods that smithwork attained to its highest perfection.

Ironwork of all kinds follows the forms of the different styles, but the transition from one style to another is slower than with other arts, and the highly imaginative lines of Late Gothic lasted well into the Renaissance, especially in Germany.

Some students have maintained that there are two different phases in the development of smithcraft, one of a more decorative character, the other architectural or tectonic. And this seems to be a correct view. But this division is equally applicable to any branch of arts and crafts. These two phases are as old as ornamental art itself. The decorative aims at enriching a surface, the tectonic limits itself to the outline or spacing of surface. The former is more dynamic and vivid, the latter more static, and gives the impression of weight and solidity. Both are best represented in their diverse characters by Late Gothic in the north, and by Renaissance in the south. Baroque and Rococo seem to unite both phases. The vertical bars of gates, for instance, represent the static and tectonic elements, whereas the frame-work, particularly the crest with its interlacing scrolls, stands for the dynamic. The different artistic conceptions obtaining in various countries have ample scope for expression in the treatment of the frame-work. The vivid forms of the north preponderate in Late Gothic, Late Baroque, and Rococo, in contradistinction to the static tectonic forms of Italian and French classical art. In the latter periods the vertical and horizontal bars are enclosed in a frame displaying a wealth of scroll, and other ornamental work. In former periods the frame was the element of stability which enclosed the richly ornamented panel in rectangular lines. Later on the reverse is the case.

The panel is now the tectonic element, the frame on the other hand the dynamic. The overthrow of gates is surmounted by a crest of the most florid character, and from it scrolls and tendrils radiate in all directions.

A later development introduces a third dimension by means of the plastic treatment of the ornament, although the lineal element is never totally absent. This phase of smithcraft is at its best in the railings, grilles, and balustrades embellishing the great Late Baroque and Rococo French, English, and German sacred and profane architectural masterpieces. The same rule applies to wrought-iron, and to stucco, wood, and stone ornament; namely that the frame is an essential part of the whole, but at the same time aims at enhancing the plastic impression of the panels. However, we should remember that decorative smithing was inspired by graphic art in its widest sense. Ornament in smithcraft depended on the decorative designs invented by the draughtsman. In the Gothic period the smiths chiefly drew their inspiration from illuminated manuscripts. This is evident in the metal work on the western doors of Notre Dame in Paris which was copied from the illuminated margins and initials embellishing manuscripts dating from the period of St. Louis. The whole surface is covered with large and small tendrils, flower sprays, leafage, and rosettes, the effect of which is both harmonious and classically restrained; in fact the panels and frame-work are nearly inseparably merged. One is almost tempted to consider the restraint of the classical ornament, formed by the sequence of ever-recurring spirals, as a Romanesque motif. Indeed, there can be little doubt that the inception of such designs dates back to the Romanesque period. But we should not forget how deeply mature Gothic in France was imbued with the classic spirit. The masters of cathedral sculptures (for instance in Rheims) very often adhered closely to antique patterns of which the drapery, the well-shaped heads, as well as the whole bearing of the figures, are a strong proof. The sketch-book of the French architect Villard d'Honnecourt, dating from the 13th century, has preserved various examples which lead us to conclude that they are based on archaeological studies of classical statues. Probably similar drawings served as models for the master-smiths when the Gothic was at its maturest period. But the majority doubtlessly took their models from illuminated manuscripts.

Mediaeval illuminated manuscripts were succeeded by calligraphic ornament during the Late Gothic period. The richly coloured illuminations were replaced by the pen-drawing pure and simple with all its wealth of curves and flourishes. The iron craftsmen now forged their rods in imitation of these calligraphic designs.

During the period of the Renaissance the calligraphic ornament attains to its zenith in Dürer's highly imaginative marginal embellishment of the Emperor Maximilian's prayer-book. The spirit of Late Gothic still held its own by means of its vivid designs long after the introduction of the Renaissance ornament which seeks expression in monumental and tectonic simplicity, wide canvasses and gigantic statues. The figures by Peter Visher on the tomb of St. Sebaldus, Dürer's Madonnas and Apostles, Hans Holbein the Younger's portraits, and other examples are Gothic creations, and much of the wrought-iron work of this period is Gothic, and not Renaissance. The calligraphic style of iron ornament still retains the vitality and vividness of Late Gothic designs. As long as the round bar predominated, Late Gothic art obtained among the blacksmiths' and locksmiths' guilds. The railings (circa 1570) enclosing Maximilian's tomb in the Hofkirche at Innsbruck are a product of the same spirit which inspired Dürer and his fellow-workers in designing the marginal ornament of that emperor's prayer-book. During the course of the 17th century and of the whole of the 18th century France undoubtedly led in decorative smithwork throughout Europe. Patterns were widely spread by the works of ornamental engravers. Many of the best examples of wrought-iron work perished during the wars, the general troubles of the times, and during the Revolution; much of it was re-forged to make arms. But the engravings of the period show very clearly the development of designs, especially of those at the end of the 17th and beginning of the 18th century.

Here again the masterpieces of smithcraft were not designed by the craftsmen themselves, but by architects and draughtsmen. It is true that the master-smiths, especially the French ones, published patterns of decorative smithing, but these designs were rarely their own inventions, rather were they inspired by architects and engravers. Some of the pattern books were published in the first half of the 17th century, such as La fidèle ouverture de l'art de Serrurier by Mathurien Jousse (1627, in La Flèche). But the main impetus was given by the books written about 1700. The engravings of the two Frenchmen Daniel Marot and Jean Berain were of the greatest importance for the development of wrought-iron work, as well as for many other branches of arts and crafts. The French call this style Régence. The German modification of the French designs of the period is described as ribbon-work. This ribbon-work motif affords opportunities for the peculiar riot of lines characteristic of the German masters. It may be compared with Late Gothic patterns, and with the scrolls and grotesque motifs of Early Baroque before the Thirty Years' War. Whereas the French attached great value to severe surface treatment and tectonic stability of ornamentation, the Germans again favoured a more lively surface treatment. The structural details of panel and frame are blurred by the exuberance of detail to such an extent that it is difficult to distinguish one from the other. In the same manner as the bar dominated and survived the Gothic period, so too did band-iron meet the requirements of decorative smithing in later times.

*   *   *

1. Door from Durham, Beginning of 13th Century. — 2. Door from the Abbey Church, Radford, Nothinghamshire, 13th Century. — 3. Door, Notre Dame, Orcival, near Clermont, 12th Century. — 4. Door Hinge from St. Alban's Abbey, 1160—90 (Victoria and Albert Museum). — 5. Hinge, Merton College, Oxford, End of 13th Century. — 6. Door of Hormead Church, near Buntingford. — 7. Door Ornament in Saffron Walden, Essex. — 8. Knocker on the North Door of Puy Cathedral, 11th Century.

Gothic

Smithcraft attained to its highest forms in France during the 13th century. The craftsman felt it incumbent on him to produce decorative smithing worthy of the great works of architecture, especially of the Gothic cathedrals. French style in its characteristic traits, whether in the Middle Ages or during the epoch of Le Grand Style, always betrays a rationalistic tendency both in architecture and arts and crafts. There seems to be a metaphysical idea hidden behind the vertical order of typical French cathedrals. Everything is carefully planned according to mathematical rules. Although the French, as northerners, had abandoned the tectonics of classical edifices, yet there is a certain similarity between the French cathedral and the Doric temple due to the harmonious arrangement of structural members, particularly in the interior. Indeed, we may venture to say that the Cathedral Gothic of northern France, where it originated and held sway for so long, is imbued with a classic spirit. French Gothic did not originate so much from the play of an enthusiastic imagination as from a very clear esprit technique. It was this spirit that enabled Gustav Eiffel to build his gigantic iron tower in the Champ de Mars for the International Exhibition in 1889.

Clarity and symmetry are the prevailing characteristics of the metal-work on the doors of Notre Dame in Paris, in spite of the exuberance of the ornamental spirals, leafage and tendrils. The main constructional wrought-iron bands, whose component parts are easily traced, are patterned very much along the lines of the composite pillar. From these composite parts the volutes spring, and form definite patterns above and below the bands extending over the panels, and in spite of their manifold curves are yet as restrained as the band ornament on antique vases with their spiral, ondoyant, and meander motifs. In spite of the wealth of rich ornament the total impression is distinctly that of unity and stability. Beautiful as the doors of Notre Dame Cathedral are, those wonderful specimens of smithcraft, the grille panels of Ourcamp Abbey, are still more beautiful (Pl. 4).

The lively and dynamic character of the Gothic ornament was developed in the latter part of the Middle Ages beyond the Rhine where more northern conceptions of art prevailed. They had once found expression in involved and fantastic grouping of animal motifs; a trait which is also met with in Irish illuminated manuscripts. The French tendency was to restrain that proneness towards the irregularity of motif inherent in northern art which is so absolutely opposed to the ordered character of classic art. Doubtlessly the Latin character of the French race was seeking expression in this tendency towards restraint of form. The French had already verged towards the Latin cultural sphere.

We may say that the decorative ironwork of the French master-smiths re-produced in this volume is Romanic in character, and it is typical of French smiths that, although they employ old and lively motifs, they are yet able to produce the effect of restraint and order. They adhered to the oldest motifs, namely the metal spirals springing from bundled flat bars and terminating in rosettes and leafage, from which the scroll was evolved, and thus established the connection with the antique. In these ornaments, that part of the bar forming the curves is rounded, and then hammered at its ends into leaves and rosettes. The most varied manners of forging are employed, but are kept strictly within the limits prescribed by the requirements of style and material. The most beau-tiful manifestations of form thus developed from employing genuine material are skilfully fashioned and eminently adapted to their purpose. Herein lies the great difference between them and the methods employed by the materialistic and mechanically-minded 19th century. The sane matter-of-fact spirit of these master-craftsmen saved them from overstepping the limits set by the material, in contra-distinction to their inferior imitators who neither possess the vitality nor the genius of the old masters.

When the French employed and enriched the old spiral ironwork patterns in the 13th and 14th centuries the effect was always one of restraint, even when they had not begun to imitate the antique by the employment of scrolls, leafage, grapes, and rosettes. This pronouncedly restrained treatment may be seen in some of the window-grilles in Rouen, in a northern French fender (Rouen Museum), or in the cathedral gate of Puy en Velai dating as far back as the end of the 12th century[1].

Beyond the spirals springing from the bundled flat bars and leafage scrolls, there are other variations such as S-curves and those similar to the curve in a note of interrogation. These motifs, when enclosed in a frame-work of square bars and connected to the frame by means of square links, are of a very charming appearance. The apertures are extremely narrow, and thus the purpose of enclosure and security is well served and emphasized. The continual repetition of ever-return-ing motifs betrays a decline in inventiveness, although the technical skill is as good as it ever was. Many of the gates, railings, and grilles with narrow apertures terminate in square rods with spear-heads which look like a row of armed men.

Compared with French Gothic smithcraft of the 13th century, German iron-work appears to be more primitive during the same and immediately following period. The work is coarser and more powerful, and the material is utilized to the limits of its technical possibilities. We may say that the difference between

---

[1] cf. C. Uhde, „Die Konstruktionen und die Kunstformen der Architektur", Berlin, E. Was-muth, 1911, p. 83 et seq.

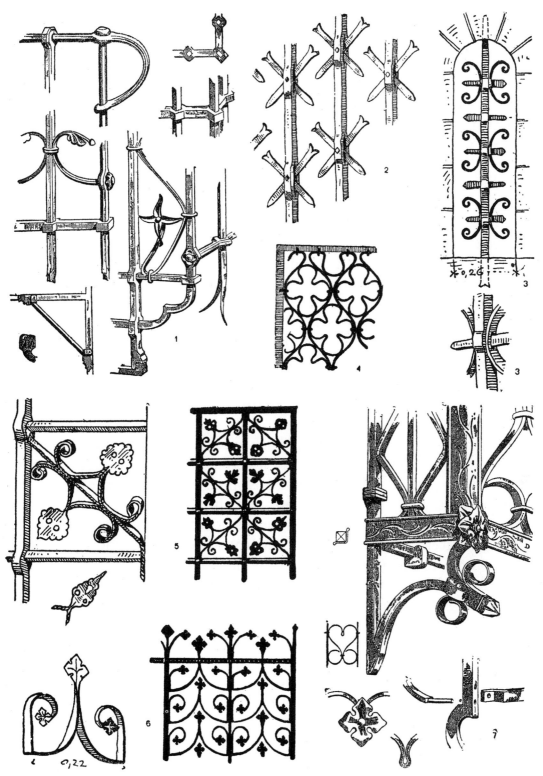

Mediaeval Railing Joints.

French and German Gothic smithcraft resembles that existing between the graceful French cathedral statue and the massive figures in the German cathedrals; for instance those of the princes and knights in the choir of Naumburg Cathedral. The classic traits are wanting in German art, on the other hand it is extremely vigorous. French art is more urbane and refined, German more rustic. French smithcraft was highly developed at a period when that of Germany was in its initial stages. But some conspicuous works already indicate promise of a high development in the future. German artists were destined to develop the Gothic along original lines, both in architecture and all branches of arts and crafts, hence also in decorative smithing.

The metal-work on doors, chests, etc., consisted chiefly of hoop-iron. Whereas in France bundled rods terminating in spirals and scroll motifs were already employed, German metal fittings still consisted of separate pieces rivetted to the wood: lattice and trellis patterns with ornamental flattened ends of a more geometrical than florid design. The C-scroll was also much favoured in Germany. Beautiful examples may be seen on a door (beginning of the 14th century) in the transept of the Abbey Church of Maulbron. Still more beautiful examples (beginning of the 13th century) are on another door of the same church. On the latter the rivets are a special feature. The general character is determined by the composition of C-scrolls, and horizontal or crossed bands arranged thus (—) (+).

In England this C-scroll is also often met with in connection with a horizontal bar, as for instance on the door of St. Margret's, Leicester. The horizontal bar is rivetted over two C-scrolls in the following manner: €€-€ (13th century). In addition, small double C-scrolls placed back to back are also frequently employed.

Door mountings attained to their greatest perfection on both sides of the Rhine during the Gothic period. The further development of decorative smithing was devoted to railings, gates, and grilles, etc., which call for other view-points and ideas. The railings are ornamented with motifs borrowed from architecture, especially from the tracery of the cathedral and church clustered and rose-windows. From now on the round is preferred to the flat bar, but the square is employed particularly for defensive purposes. The spirals, S- and C-scrolls are replaced by the quatrefoil forged in square and round bars. Thus the favourite motif of the stone-mason is adopted by the blacksmith. The development of tracery-work brought about by the inventiveness of the stone-masons is copied by the decorative smiths when ornamenting their gate and door panels. The flamboyant tracery which became popular during the Late Gothic period is also transferred to ironwork, and usually framed in a circle. The earlier severity is replaced by lively motifs. This rayonnant and flamboyant style, which is chiefly found in the 14th and the beginning of the 15th century in French cathedral rose-windows, is also transferred to iron-work. The motifs are often as delicate as lace or fret-saw work. In many cases the ornament has been sawn or filed into the iron. The details often appear coarse and carelessly executed. The chief aim seems to have been to create a general impression, and this results in a hazy, restless composition. In such cases the bars are hardly distinguishable. Hence ironwork treated in this manner could not continue along the same line of development. Round or square bars placed horizontally or vertically, or com-bined to form a trellis, supplied the first patterns and form the base for all further modifications.

Italian and French Railings, 13th and 14th Centuries

1. Langeac Church, Chapel Railings, Upper Part, About 1400. — 2. St. Mark's, Venice (gilded),
13th Century. — 3 and 4. Verona, Tombs of the Scaligers, 1300—1380 (Total Height About 2,6 metres. —
5 and 6. Town Hall, Siena, 14th Century. — 7. French Tabernacle Railings (gilded), 14th Century. —
8. French, 13th Century (?), in the Museum of Decorative Arts, Paris. — 9. From Brescia, 14th Century.

Late Gothic and Renaissance

The predominance of the linear pattern in decorative smithing among the transalpine peoples is particularly conspicuous when we regard the more plastically conceived ironwork of the Italians. It is true that the influence of the purely Gothic conception lingered on in Italy till well into the 15th century (Quattrocento). The Italians were also appreciative of the Late Gothic linear pattern for which the employment of iron was so well adapted. But the Italians introduced the architectural element to a much greater extent than did the northern craftsmen. The southern architects had begun to develop a more perfect sense of proportion. And in doing so the great masters, such as Brunelleschi, Leonbattista Alberti, Bramante, and many others, harked back to classical architecture.

A palace or the dome of a church over a central plan was always regarded by the Italians from a purely plastic point of view, and the beautiful proportions of Italian buildings still charm us to-day as do the Doric columns of a Greek temple. It is therefore by no means a matter of surprise that the Italians should treat ornamental details more plastically than the craftsmen of northern countries. The effect of the pondrous window-grilles in the ground-floors of the palaces is essentially plastic. They consist of crossed square interpenetrated bars of considerable dimensions, and are very picturesque in their massive strength. Hence the effect is not produced by the simple line itself, but by the bulkiness of the material employed. In the Gothic period, the chief stress then was laid on linear effects, whereas in the Italian Renaissance decorative smithing had become distinctly plastic, and this is still more the case with Baroque and Rococo ironwork.

Besides the window-grilles, it was above all the finely smithed lamp-holders supporting a cradle and ring, torch-holders, and lanterns that provided considerable scope for plastic treatment of Italian ironwork. For instance the celebrated lanterns on the Palazzo Guadagni in Florence look like small tabernacles, and are minute replicas of the great centrally-planned octagonal edifices. Indeed, as is well-known, the centrally-planned building was the most favoured during the Italian Renaissance, and the superstructure on the dome is actually called a lantern. The lamps on the Italian palace façades are not different in shape to the lanterns crowning the circular and octagonal centrally-planned buildings. Pillars and pilasters, all of minute dimensions, were also the main tectonic elements of these ornamental lanterns. Each of the eight openings are arcaded, and there is also a miniature balustrade of pillars with a richly ornamented rail on top, and small breaks at the corners. The whole is crowned by large spikes, of which the middle ones are straight and the corner ones curved outwards.

In the case of torch-holders, door-knockers, and other similar pieces of metal furniture, casting was often resorted to in order to secure the desired plastic

Details of German Renaissance Railings.

effect. And there can be no doubt that the masterpieces of cast bronze and embossed work, as perfected by the sculptors of the q u a t t r o c e n t o, such as Lorenzo Ghiberti, Donatello, and Verrocchio supplied the necessary and natural patterns for smithcraft. Verrocchio himself produced his finest work on the bronze screen in the Old Sacristy of San Lorenzo in Florence. This screen is made in imitation of coiled ropes, and the acanthus ornament on the sarcophagus (also by Verrocchio) near the screen may have served as a model for later smithcraft work.

Many examples of ironwork show how the Italian blacksmiths aimed at highly plastic effects. The curves and spirals north of the Alps during the 15th and 16th centuries contrast greatly with this plastic Renaissance ironwork. And they can only be explained by the fact that the Gothic spirit with its preference for linear motifs still prevailed there. Whereas in Italy the architects and sculptors influenced decorative smithing, it was the graphic artists Martin Schongauer and Albrecht Dürer who exercised the main influence north of the Alps during this period. There is every indication that the handicrafts guilds were influenced almost too long by Albrecht Dürer's spirit and Late Gothic examples.

The peculiar alternating influence exercised by Late Gothic and Renaissance, which is so conspicuous in all Dürer's works, may be traced more or less in German art during the 16th century. Maximilian's tomb in the Hofkirche in Innsbruck is an example of the influence of two style epochs. Now the figures by Peter Vischer are Renaissance masterpieces, and hardly less plastic than Italian Renaissance sculptures, but the railings round the tomb, which were completed in 1570, are absolutely the product of the Late Gothic spirit obtaining in the north. This may readily be seen by the linear motifs. The curved motifs developed from the figure eight, formed by means of interpenetrated round bars which fill the panels of the railings, are reminiscent of calligraphic flourishes. But although Gothic vivacity still prevails, there is a suggestion of Renaissance restraint. The scroll motif with foliage, vine, and other leaves betrays supreme artistic skill. The railing with its round bars enriched by crocket ornament is a masterpiece of Gothic ironwork. Other prominent examples of Gothic iron⸗ work favour drawn⸗out spindle⸗shaped spirals tapering at the ends; they may be compared with the twists of a corkscrew, and were shaped on a wooden peg which was afterwards burnt out. This method was employed in producing various other patterns in wrought⸗iron, especially in Spain, where bars were hammered onto a wooden background which was then burnt, leaving a trellis or lattice. This is again a proof of how closely mountings, trellis, and lattice⸗ work are connected in their technical origins. The spindle⸗shaped spirals may be regarded as an attempt to treat the linear round bars plastically. But com⸗ pared with Italian Renaissance wrought ironwork the attempt is but feeble.

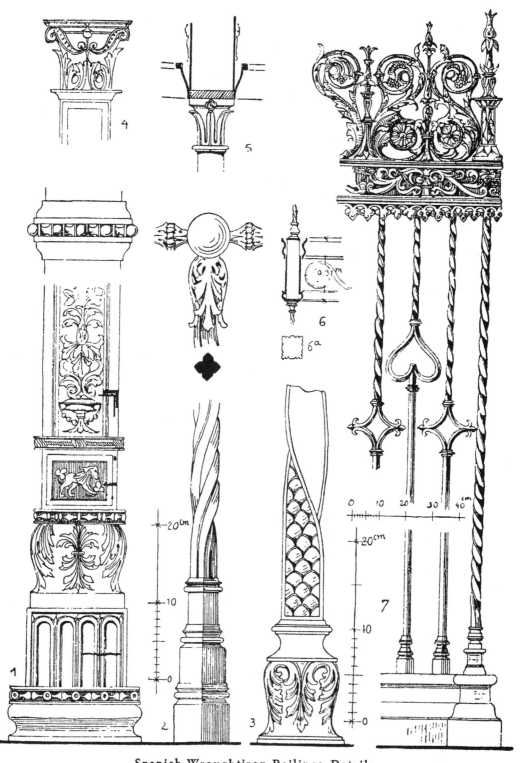

Spanish Wroughtiron Railings. Details.

1 and 2. Cuenza Cathedral, Railings of the Capilla major, Details of Lower Part. — 3, 4, 5. Cuenza Cathedral, Part of the Railings behind the High Altar, by Sanchos Muñez. — 6. Toledo Cathedral, Railings of the Holy Ghost Chapel, by Domingo Cespedes (1529); 6a. Profile of the Twisted Bars. — 7. Siguenza Cathedral, Chapel Railings (1530).

There are a great number of examples of the different modes of smithing iron. Space does not permit of giving details of all the great masterpieces. The illus‹ trations in this volume afford a sufficiently comprehensive survey. The main object of this introduction is to but touch on a few style problems.

We should remember that it was not Germany alone which laid the chief stress on linear and surface effects of wrought‹iron ornament. Nearly all other European countries have produced masterpieces of this type. And even Italy, in spite of her many examples of purely plastic ornamental smithcraft, also turned out excellent work of a linear character made of round bars, or, a peculiar ltalian pattern, of flat ones with the thin edge turned outward. But Italian ironworkers favour different decorative motifs, and as a rule dislike the peculiar calligraphic flourishes of the northern countries. The S‹curve takes the place of the spiral. When the S‹scroll motifs are employed in Germany they are so closely grouped that the effect is almost net‹like (*e. g.* the railings of Ambras Castle). And we may remark here that the impression created by Italian line ornament has none of the restlessness so characteristic of the northern Late Gothic with its h o r r o r v a c u i, which led to the filling up of every available space and gap. The wide spacing of Italian ornament is an important factor in the clearness and restraint of the pattern. And although Italian linear railings, for instance, are not conceived as integral architectural parts of the edifices they embellish, nevertheless the general impression is thoroughly static and tectonic. And this is in accordance with the artistic intentions of southern Renaissance ideals.

The Spaniard, like the German, also favoured a close grouping of his orna‹ ment. And, indeed, we may say that Spanish and German art approach very near in spirit, especially during the Late Gothic and Late Baroque periods. With Spanish art, of course, the tradition of the East is still very noticeable. And we should remember that the filling of every available space was a peculiar Oriental trait. There is something reminiscent of the Oriental carpet and rug patterns in these closely‹packed Spanish examples of ornamental iron smithing. Whereas Italian wrought ironwork is classic in its simplicity, the effect of Spanish smithing is almost impressionistic by reason of the hazy effect produced by the peculiar grouping and crowding of the motifs. Eminent examples of the peculiar Spanish treatment of metalwork are the screens in the churches that surround the long narrow choirs. They project into the crossing and nave and separate the clergy from the congregation.

Of course it is but natural that Italian art has its tap‹roots in classic traditions, and always returns to them: whereas Spanish art is strongly influenced, as we have seen, by Oriental examples due to historical events, and northern art perpetually betrays that peculiar restlessness which after all is the outcome of a certain element of romanticism. Hence Spain on the one hand, and the countries north of the Alps on the other had to overcome their inherent conceptions of art before they succumbed to the all-absorbing influence of the classic spirit to which their traditions were opposed. But, nevertheless, as far as smithcraft is concerned, Italy did not remain the leader of classic art. The a r s n o v a did not pass straight from Italy to Germany and the northern countries, but found its way there from France who soon assumed the leadership in smithcraft and continued to develop classic traditions into which she, however, projected a completely new spirit by turning her main attention to the architectural effect of castle gates with their imposing piers.

The French smith put his best work into the development of the g r i l l e d ' h o n n e u r. The classic models imported from Italy still form the base of the ornament, but undergo modifications making for a peculiar refinement of patterns and motifs which were later imitated by the Germans. But there as well as in France the centres of art were the courts, and the spirit of these absolutistic courts of the Baroque period was naturally reflected in the smithcraft which they did so much to perfect by their patronage. It is a moot question whether the Baroque or the classic tradition is the most pronounced in the g r i l l e d ' h o n n e u r.

Railing from Florence, 15th Century.

Italian and French Railings, 16th Century

Baroque and Classicism

France introduces a new tectonic principle into her main gates, namely a vertical order with uninterrupted rows of mighty square bars. The whole surface is divided vertically. Though there is a certain amount of ornament between the verticals, the ornament is gradually concentrated on the overthrow in order not to mar the general impression of verticality. But the base of the overthrow is usually curved. The severity of the vertical lines in the gates-proper, combined with the lively ornamental work on the piers and overthrow, make for a very decorative whole. Altogether the architectural element predominates, and the ornamental details are only of secondary importance, thus following the law of architecture according to which embellishment must always be subordinated to tectonic requirements. Where the Baroque style is fully expressed in ironwork the effect of railings and gates as enclosures of the more important edifices is such that the impression of seclusion is very pronounced. The gates are mostly placed in such a manner as to afford charming perspectives of the enclosed edifice. Owing to the semicircular overthrow the impression is created that the gates constitute an outwardly projecting bay that seems almost to encircle the castle or mansion to which it gives entrance. Herein lies one of the supreme accomplishments of Baroque art.

The scroll and leafage ornaments are partly conventionalized, partly realistically treated. The ribbon-work motif is also favoured. — An example of Early Baroque may be seen on Plate 126. Its effect is somewhat primitive. The leading motif is presented by the square bars set rather far apart. Curved bands supply the place of horizontal bars in the middle and above. The intervening space is filled with vine-leaves and tendrils, these latter are an echo of the spindle ornament. Nevertheless, the general impression is one of sketchiness, although there is no blurring of the tectonic and decorative elements. The more important examples are richer in decorative motifs, and the linear element is replaced by the plastic, and this plastic feature is continually added to in the course of time. A noteworthy example of perfect workmanship should be mentioned here, namely the grille d'honneur from the Château Maison Lafitte now in the Louvre. The gates are good representative examples of the grand style of the 17th century. The French railings and gates assume huge proportions, especially those surrounding the great cours d'honneur of the castles and hôtels which they serve both to protect and embellish. It is well to remark that the railings and gates were interpreted as belonging architecturally to the façade, at least they harmonized to an extraordinary degree with the buildings. The artistic problem which had to be solved was, that in spite of the space between the edifice and the surrounding railings and gates, the effect of unity had to be produced, and was produced. Square bars with lance-heads and tassels were much favoured, and were the main features of the gates. Sometimes the overthrow consisted of a richly moulded cornice with a pyramid of highly ornamental scroll-work surmounted by the royal arms and crown, or other heraldic emblems, supported by pronouncedly plastic and florid foliage ornament. However luxuriant these overthrows may be, they do not, as might be supposed, reduce the static effect of the vertical plan.

No doubt the stately gates and railings at Versailles served as an example for much of the decorative smithing at this period, just as the castles built by Jules Hardouin Mansard, and the gardens laid out by André Le Nôtre were patterns for architects and landscape gardeners throughout Europe. The influence of Versailles is particularly noticeable in England, where French masters were employed by the court and aristocracy, and created such masterpieces as Jean Tijon's magnificent screen of wrought-iron at Hampton court, perhaps the finest piece of decorative smithing in the world.

Ironwork in France during the period of Louis XIV. was still very much influenced by the traditions of the Renaissance as is quite evident by its severe restraint. During the Régence, however, this trait gave way to an exuberance of motifs which was increased still more during the Rococo period, i. e. the time covering the reign of Louis XV. The greatest masterpieces of this style epoch are the celebrated gates and railings enclosing the Place Stanislas in Nancy. They were made by Jean Lamours, the court smith of King Stanislas Lescynski. The main trait of the preceding period, namely the stressing of the tectonic character of ironwork, especially of railings and gates, is still markedly evident in Lamours' work. Wherever architectural requirements call for pillars or other supports, the bars are either closely grouped or bundled. A similar arrangement is met with in the trellised garden-houses of the period. These too are essentially architectural features in the grounds, and are in perfect harmony with the surroundings; both buildings and landscape.

The iron gates and railings in the Place Stanislas in Nancy accord so beautifully with their setting that it would be difficult to find their equal anywhere. The railings are purely tectonic, the frame and overthrows mainly serve ornamental requirements, but the whole is arranged so skilfully that the railings and gates seem to be an integral part of the surrounding edifices, and this is especially emphasized where there are gaps between the houses, in which case the railings appear to connect them, and thus make the gaps part of the rhythm of the whole. At this point we may remark that town-planning does not merely mean planting houses at given intervals, and on particular spots, but it means the creation of an artistic ensemble. In Nancy the iron craftsman has contributed to this requirement by the beauty and utility of his work. The modern town-planner would do well to remember how much may be done by such work as distinguishes the Place Stanislas.

The object of the railings and gates surrounding the Place Stanislas is of course to enclose, but as they do not form a wall, there is no obstruction of the view, and light and air are not excluded. This, of course, accords with the general tendency of the Rococo period, namely to provide large windows flush with the walls, and thus flood the buildings with light. Decorative plastic figures are placed in the portal-like gates. The square itself is embellished with fountains with bombé basins. The railings follow the outline of the square, but are rounded at the corners. The ornamental details surmounting the railings are replete with rocaille patterns which are so beautifully formed that they are in no way inferior to the stuccos and wood-carvings of the Rococo period. Nevertheless, the general impression is perfectly harmonious, in spite of the multitude of details. Similar railings, but with somewhat lighter overthrows, were also smithed in Germany; for instance in Würzburg.

Gradually the exuberance of the rocaille ornament was toned down. The vertical line began to dominate again, and a more classic spirit becomes evident. This phase of Late Baroque is usually called Louis XVI, of which wonderful examples exist in the grilles d'honneur in front of the large courtyards of the great monumental French edifices. The tectonic element again comes to the fore. The ornament, instead of being curved, is angular. The spiral is replaced by the meander. The frame and piers are now only embellished with plain circles similar to those in the heavy gates of the Château Maison Lafitte. The grand style and the style of Louis XVI. are akin in form. With the latter the piers consist of huge square rods. Heavily moulded cornices surmount the gates. The railings terminate in lance-heads, with or without tassels. There is something distinctly reserved in the character of these railings which is enhanced by the emphatic manner in which they cut off the grounds and edifices they surround from the rest of the world. Good examples are those outside the Palace of Justice and the Military School in Paris.

German examples of ironwork comparable with the railings surrounding the Place Stanislas may be seen in the gates and railings in front of the castle in Würzburg. The railings are not carried along a straight line, but are curved. Intervening stone piers and sentry-boxes capped by obelisks afford the necessary supports. The verticality of the bars is blurred by a wealth of ornament and embellishment, above all the overthrows abound in rocaille motifs. Sometimes the bars are placed in such a manner as to improve the perspective, for instance in the panels of the railings at Weingarten Monastery, as well as at Zwiefalten, and in the shrine of Maria Einsiedeln in Switzerland. The central-piece of the choir-screen at Zwiefalten is constructed in such a manner that the Virgin and Jesus, who are completely surrounded by a golden halo, seem to be set in the niche of an altar. Hence it will be seen that smithcraft was able to produce the illusion of perspective on a flat surface in accordance with the style requirements of the period. During the Louis XVI. period the Germans imitated French models. Finally, wrought-iron was replaced by inferior cast-iron work. In the age of machinery ornamental smithcraft fell gradually into disuse, and it has not yet been revived to any appreciable extent.

The illustrations are reproduced from photographs of the following publishing firms:

Alinari, Florence
    Plates 22, 23, 24, 31, 43, 63, 64, 65, 67, 68, 69, 86, 87, 92, 93, 97, 98, 99.
Brogi, Florence
    Plates 21.
Giraudon, A., Paris
    Plates 7, 18, 126, 137, 185, 216, 312.
Laurent y Cia, Madrid
    Plates 2, 3, 74, 75, 76, 77, 78, 79, 80, 81, 82, 83, 84, 85.
Moscione, Rome
    Plates 96, 180.
Müller, Christof, Nürnberg
    Plates 44, 47, 102, 108, 116, 131.
Austrian State Photographic Department, Vienna I
    Plates 27, 28, 29, 34, 54, 57, 107, 152, 153, 156, 157, 158, 159, 175, 220, 221, 222, 223, 224, 225,
    231, 232, 233, 234, 235, 236, 237, 244, 245, 246, 254, 279, 280, 281, 285, 286, 304, 311, 316.
Poppi, Bologne
    Plates 306.
Reusch, August, Munich
    Plates 36, 38, 39, 40, 41, 48, 53, 111, 150, 154, 174, 252, 253, 255, 283, 304.
From: H. R. d'Allemagne, Ferronnerie anciennne, Paris 1924
    Plates 5, 6, 31, 95, 190.
From: Contet, F., Documents de Ferronnerie ancienne, Paris 1922
    Plates 1.

*   *   *

The publishers wish to express their gratitude to the Director of the Victoria and Albert
Museum for kind permission to reproduce several illustrations.

THE PLATES

1. France, 12th century—Screen with Door (Detail). The Cathedral, Puy

2. Spain, 12th century—Door Furniture in Marcevols Abbey

3. Spain, 13th century—Screen with Door. The Cathedral, Palencia

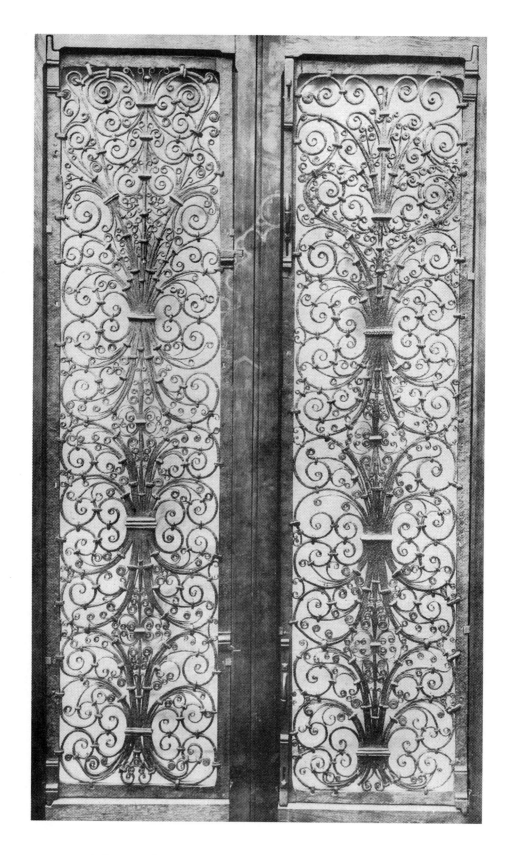

4. France, 13th century—Grille Panels from Ourscamp Abbey
Musée Le Secq des Tournelles, Rouen

5. France, 13th century—Detail of Grille Panel from Ourscamp Abbey

6. France, 13th century—Grille Panel. Musée Le Secq des Tournelles, Rouen

7. France, 13th century—Grille Decorations in Wrought Iron. Musée des Arts Décoratifs, Paris

8. France, 13th century—1) and 3) Railings; 2) Mounting of a Door

9. France, second half of the 13th century—Oak Coffer, with Wrought Iron Scrollwork
Victoria and Albert Museum, London

10. Liège, 13th century—Door, formerly St. Paul's Church, now Archaeological Museum

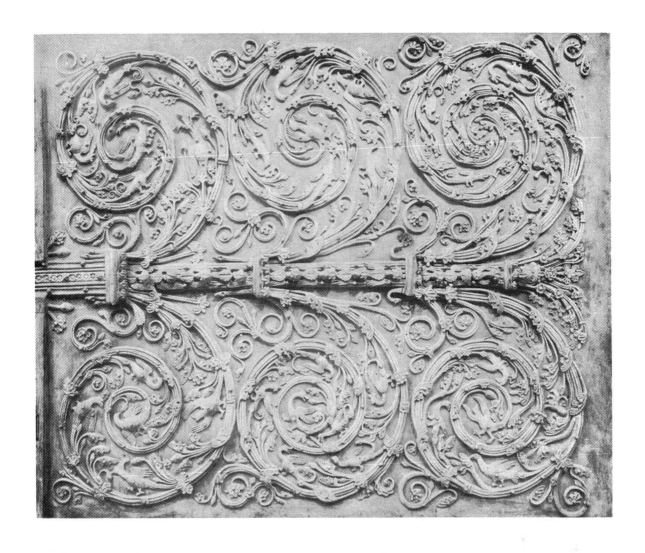

11. France, 13th century—Door Mountings. 1) Notre Dame, Paris; 2) Saint Gilles Cathedral

12. France, 13th century—Door Mounting on the West Front of the Paris Cathedral

13. Germany, first half of the 14th century—Doors. The Cathedral, Erfurt

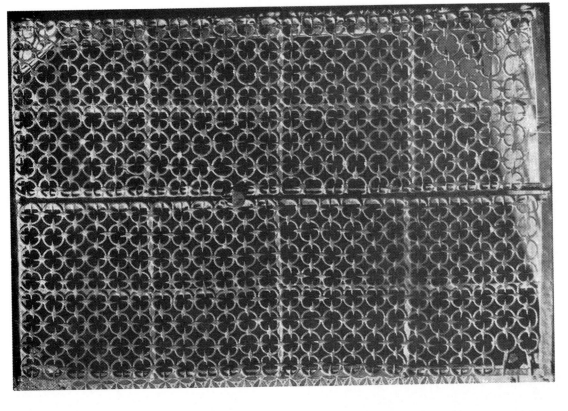

14. France and Italy, 13th and 14th centuries—Screens

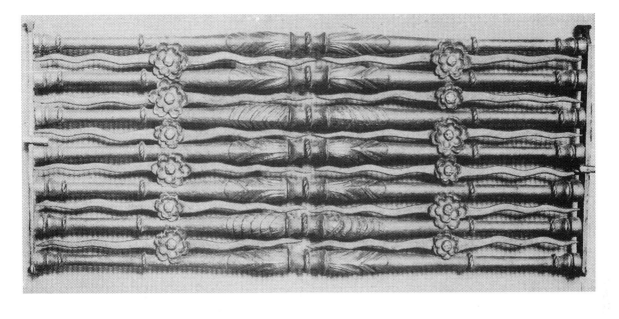

15. Germany and France, 14th century—Screens

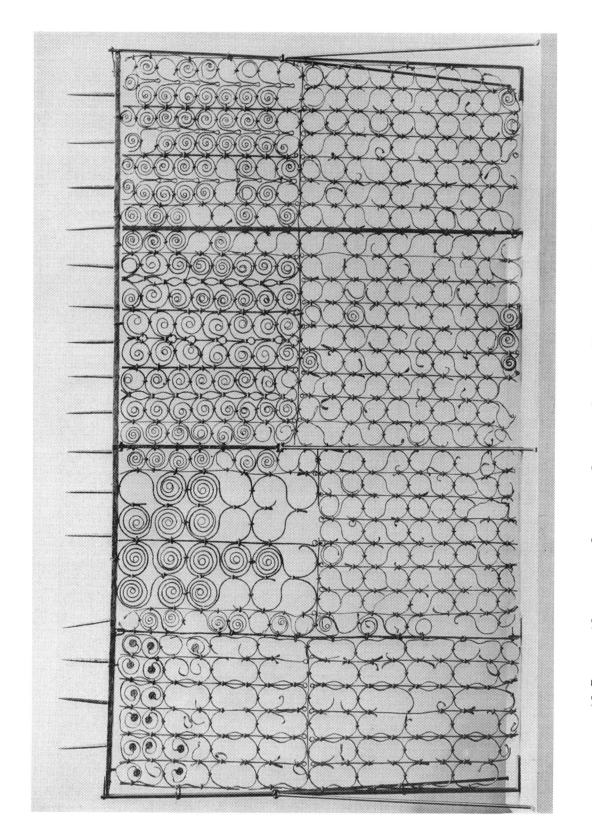

16. England, 13th century—Screen from Chichester Cathedral. Victoria and Albert Museum, London

17. England, late 14th or early 15th century—Lower Part of a Pair of Gates
Victoria and Albert Museum, London

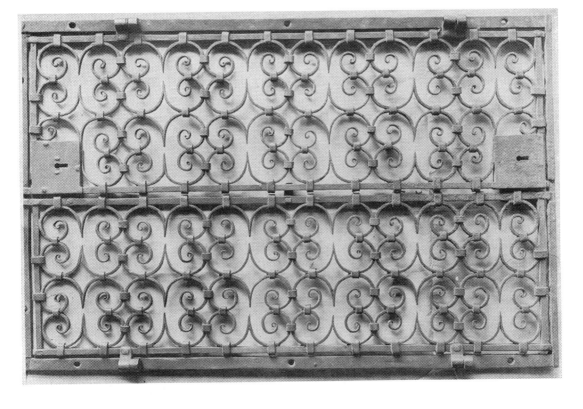

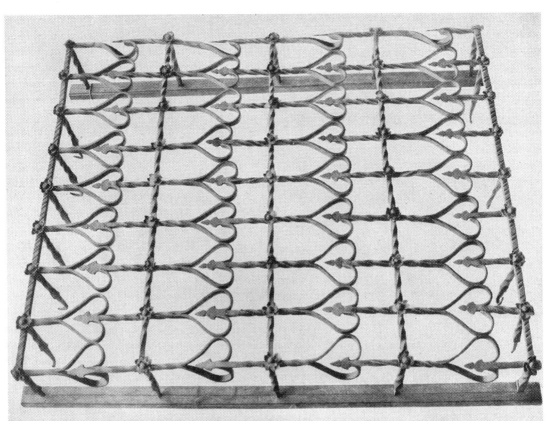

18. France—Left: 14th century, Window Grille, from Bourges. Right: 15th century, Gates, Musée des Arts Décoratifs, Paris

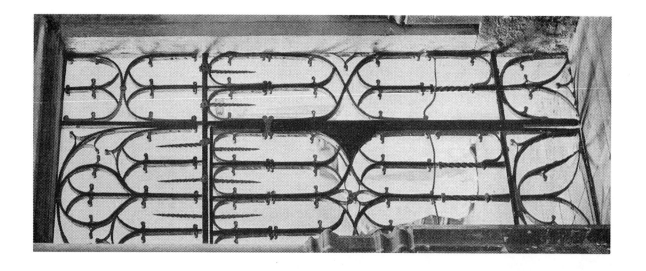

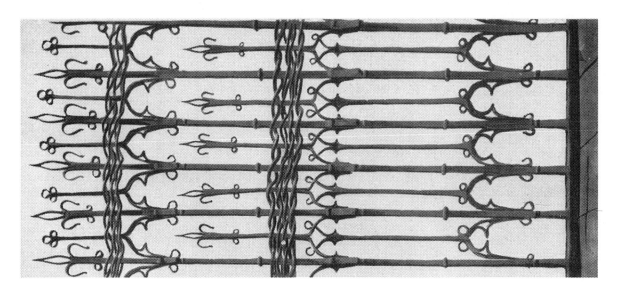

19. France and Flanders, 15th century—Gothic Screens

20. Italy, about 1370—Screen. Santa Croce, Florence

21. Italy, about 1380—Screen. Tombs of the Scaligeri, Verona

22. Italy, about 1400—Screen in the Palazzo Publico, Siena

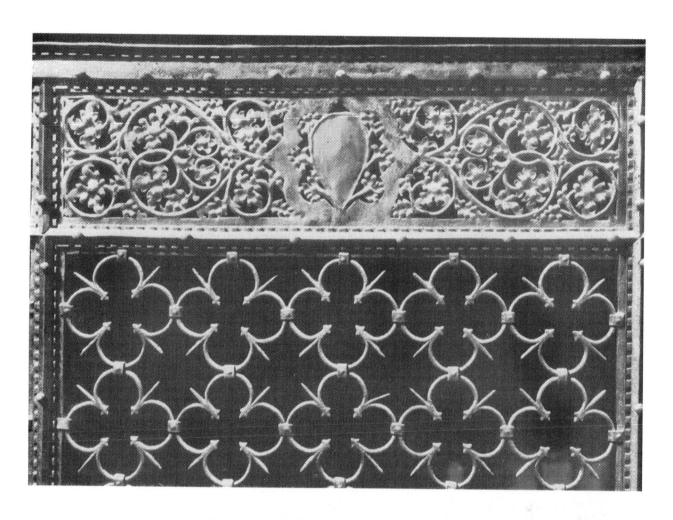

23. Italy—Above: Screen, about 1400. Santa Trinita, Florence; Below: Small Box of Iron, 15th century, Siena

24. Florence, 14th century, and Austria, 15th century—Grating and Door with Pierced Iron Work Panels

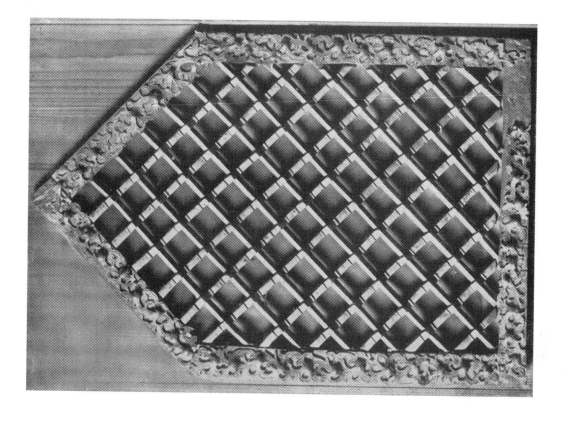

25. Austria, 15th century—Grating and Door of Tabernacle

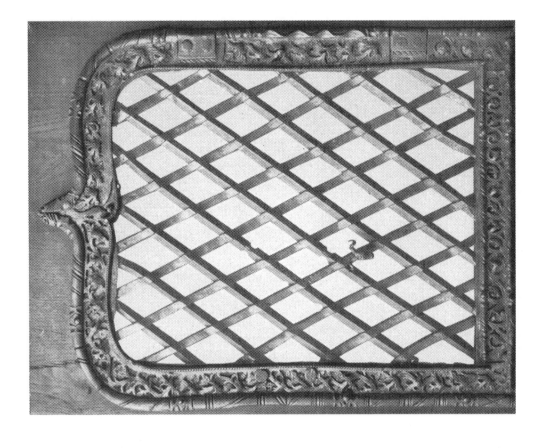

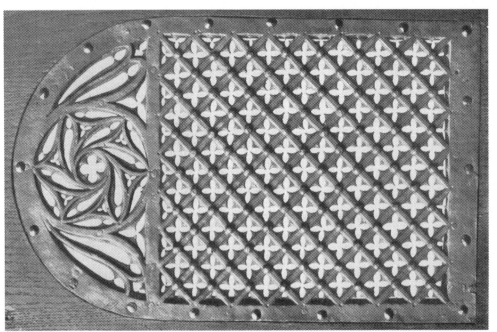

26. Germany, 15th century—Gratings. Museum of Arts and Crafts, Hamburg

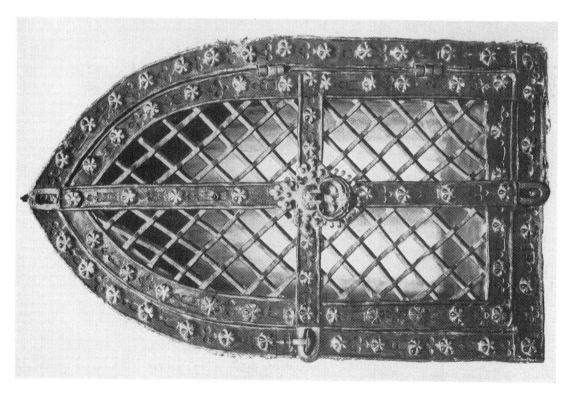

27. Austria, 15th century—Grating—Grating of Tabernacle. France, 15th century—Grating

28. Austria, 15th century—Door of the Tabernacle in the Spitalkirche, Krems

29. Austria, 15th century—Door of the Tabernacle in the Spitalkirche, Krems

30. Netherlands, 15th century—Grille. Victoria and Albert Museum, London

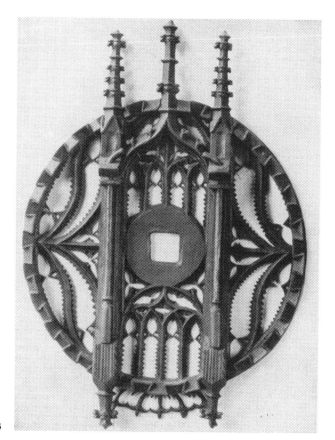

31. 1 and 4) France, 15th century—Gratings; 2) Netherlands, 15th century—Door of Tabernacle
3) France, 15th century—Part of Knocker

32. Austria, 15th century—Detail from Tabernacle and Sacristy Door

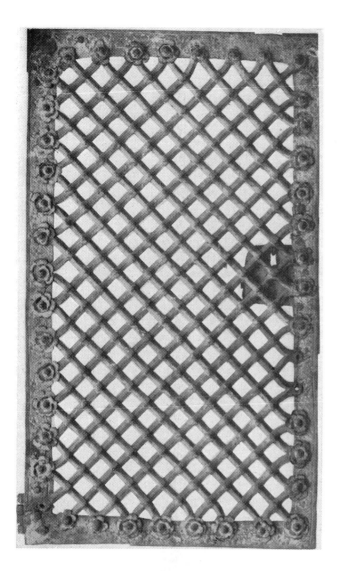

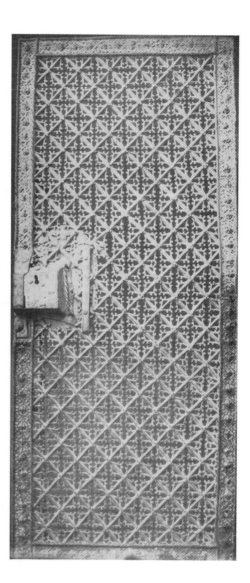

33. Germany, late 15th century—Doors and a Grille Panel in Wrought Iron

34. Austria, 15th century—Door of the Maria-Stiegen Church, Vienna

35. Hungary, 15th century—Church Door at Lápis-Patak

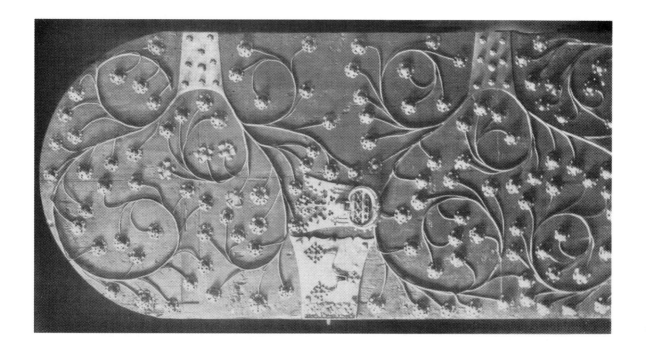

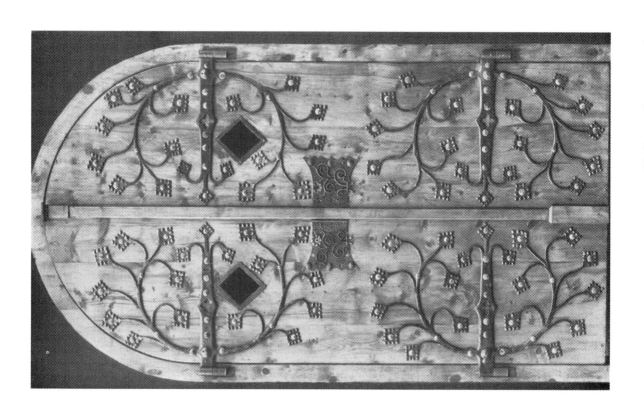

36. South Germany, 15th century—Door Furniture

37. Germany, 15th century—Door Furniture. Germanic Museum, Nuremberg

38. South Germany, 15th century—Hinges

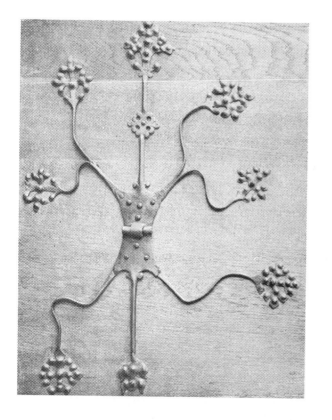

39. South Germany, 15th century—Hinges and other Door Furniture

40. South Germany, 15th century—Door Mounting

41. South Germany, 15th century—Door Mounting

42. France, 15th century—Locks

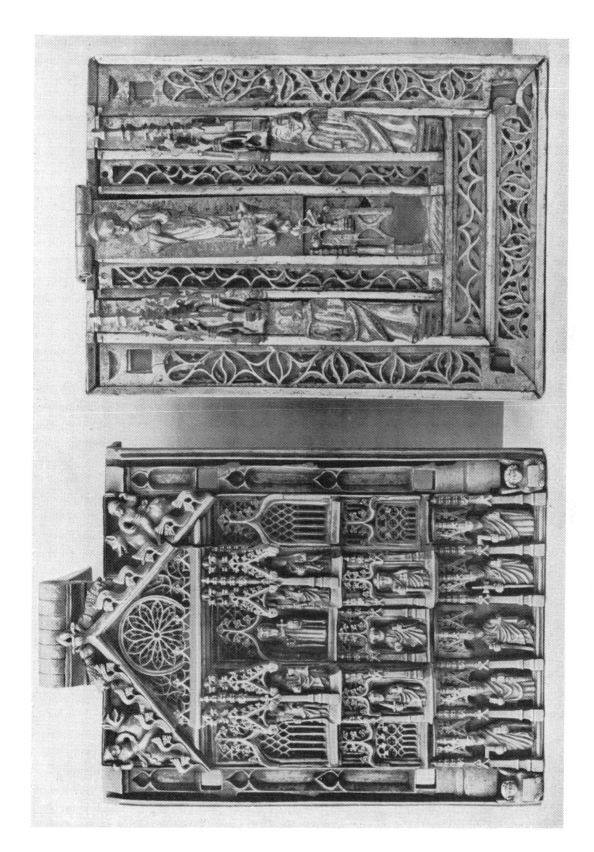

43. France, 15th century—Locks. Cluny Museum, Paris

44. Germany, late 15th century—Mountings of Locks. Germanic Museum, Nuremberg

45. Germany, 1450–1500—Knocker and Door Mountings. National Museum, Munich

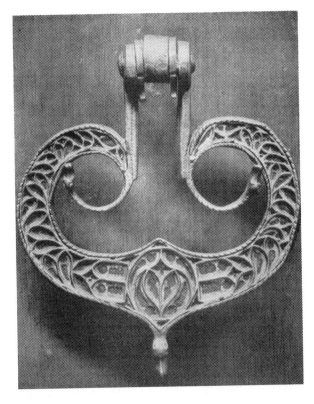

46. Germany, 15th century—Door Knockers

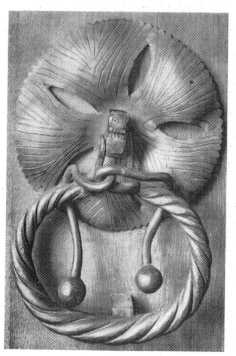 

47. Germany, 15th century—Door Handle and Door Knockers

48. South Germany, 16th century—Door with Iron Mounting

49. Germany, 16th century—Door with Iron Mounting, Nuremberg Work

50. Switzerland, 15th century—Door Handles. Historical Museum, Bâle

51. Switzerland, 15th century—Door Handles and Hinges. Historical Museum, Bâle

52. Germany, 15th century—Wrought Iron Plate for a Door Handle
Germanic Museum, Nuremberg

53. South Germany, about 1500—Tabernacle of Wrought Iron
National Museum, Munich

54. Tirol, about 1500—Screen in the Parish Church in Hall, Austria

55. Germany, about 1470—Screen in the Church of St. Ulrich, Augsburg

56. Tirol, about 1500—Screen in the Parish Church in Hall, Austria

57. Tirol, about 1500—Screen in the Parish Church in Hall, Austria

58. North Brabant, late 15th century—Chandelier, Heeswyk Castle

59. Germany, 15th century—Chandelier. National Museum, Munich

60. Germany, late Gothic Bracket Candle Sconce from Zülpich Church, Rhineland

61. Germany, late 15th century—Bracket Candle Sconce
Kunstgewerbe Museum, Cologne

62. Germany, early 16th century—Candelabrum. St. John's Church, Cologne

63. Italy, 15th century—Firedogs of Wrought Iron

64. France, 15th century—1) Knocker; 2) Screen. French Work, at the Museo Nazionale, Florence

65. Spain, 16th century—Chimney Screen. Louvre, Paris

66. Spain, 1525—Pulpit in the Cathedral, Ávila

67. Italy, 15th century—Lantern on the Palazzo Guadagni, Florence

68. Italy, 15th century—Torch Holders. Left: Palazzo Grisoli; Right: Piazza Postierla, Siena

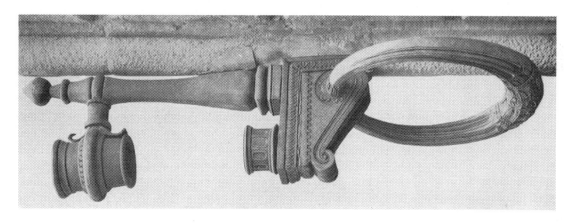

69. Italy, 15th century—Torch Holders on Florentine Palaces

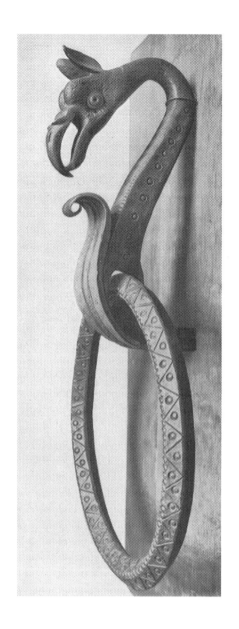

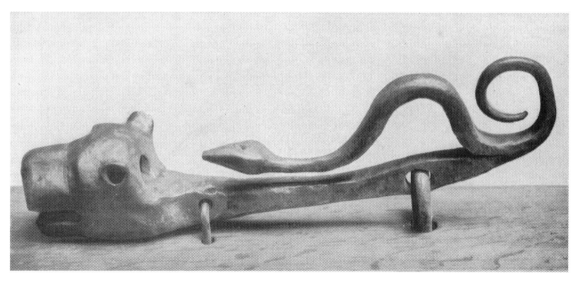

70. Italy, 15th and 16th centuries—Door Knockers. Schloss-Museum, Berlin

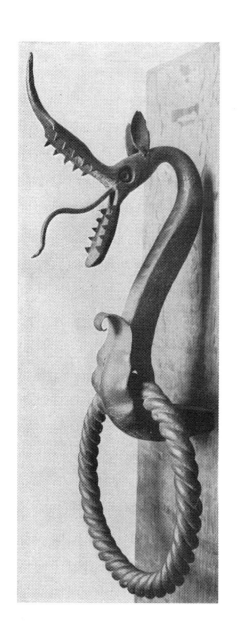

71. Italy, 15th and 16th centuries—Door Knockers. Schloss-Museum, Berlin

72. Italy, about 1500—Pair of Gates. Palazzo Bevilaqua, Bologna

73. Italy, about 1500—Balcony Balustrade. Palazzo Bevilaqua, Bologna

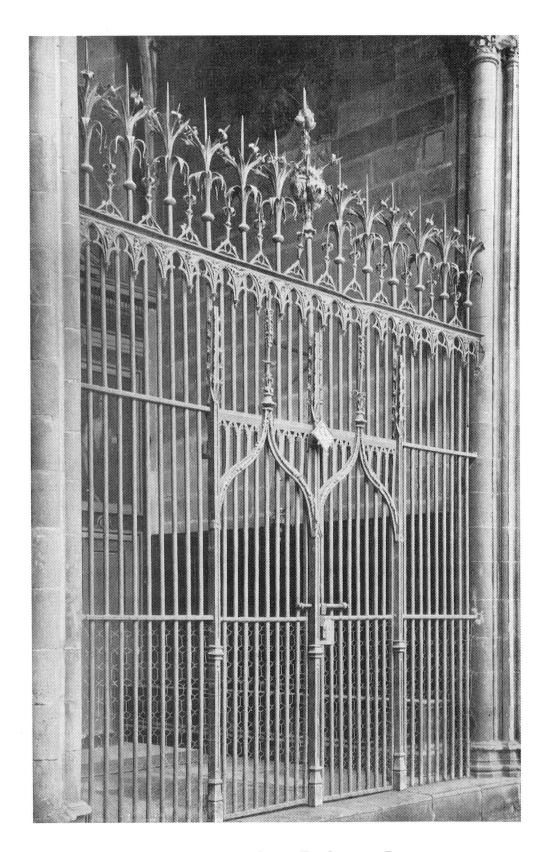

74. Spain, 15th century—Screen. The Cathedral, Barcelona

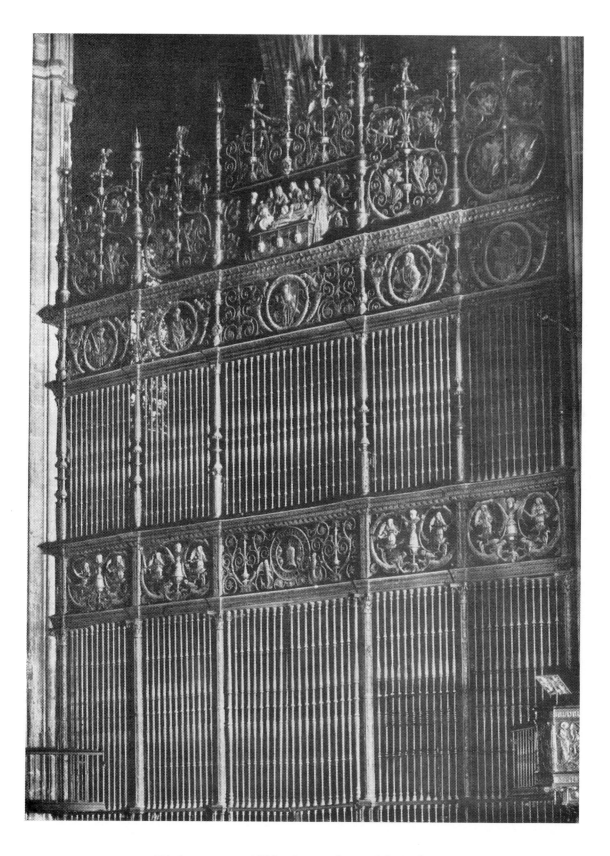

75. Spain, about 1530—Screen. Capilla Mayor, Seville

76. Spain, 16th century—Screen in the Cathedral, Placentia

77. Spain, 16th century—Altar Screen, Saragossa

78. Spain, 16th century—Church Screen, Jerez de la Fontera

79. Spain, 16th century—Screen of the Royal Chapel in the Cathedral, Granada

80. Spain, 16th century—Window Grille, Salamanca

81. Spain, 16th century—Window Grille, Salamanca

82. Spain, 16th century—Window Grille, Seville

83. Spain, about 1560—Wrought Iron Grille

84. Spain, 16th century—Chapel Screen in the Cathedral, Palencia

85. Spain, 16th century—Screen. The University, Salamanca

86. Italy, end of the 15th century—Window Grille in the Scuola di S. Giorgio, Venice

87. Italy, 15th century—Window Grating, Venice

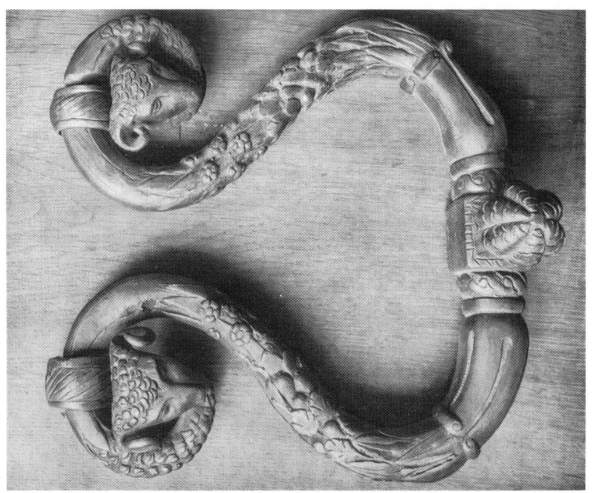

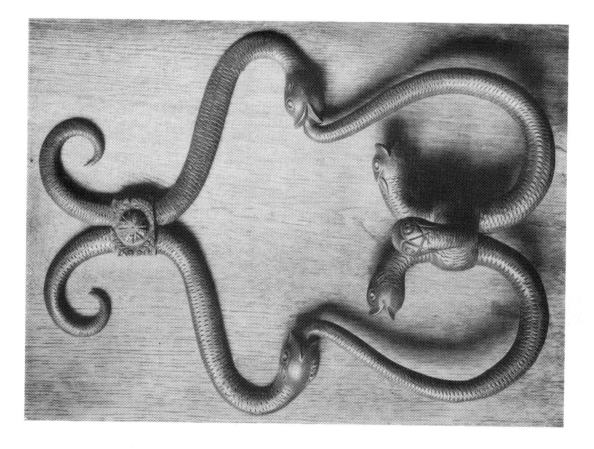

89. Door Knockers. Left: France, 16th century—Cluny Museum, Paris. Right: Italy, 16th century—Schloss-Museum, Berlin

90. France, 16th century—Grille, Rouen

91. France, 16th century—Gates, Le Mans

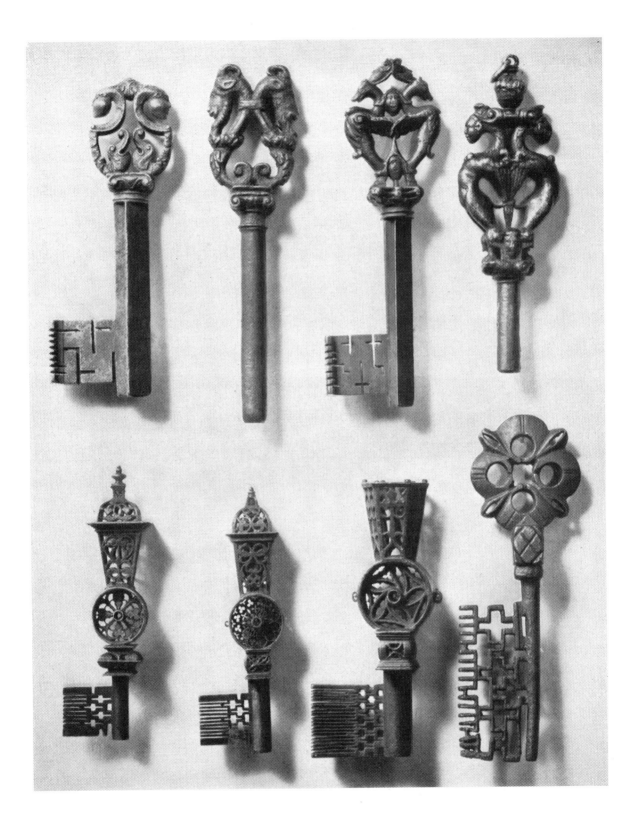

92. France, 16th century—Keys. Museo Nazionale, Florence

93. France, 16th century—Door Furniture

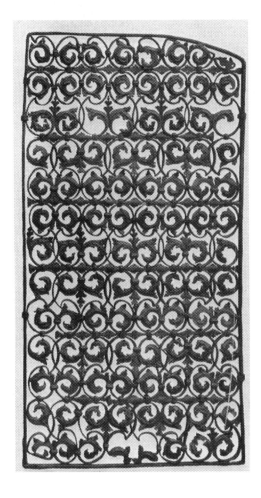

94. Italy, 16th century—Sections of Ornamental Railings. Schloss-Museum, Berlin

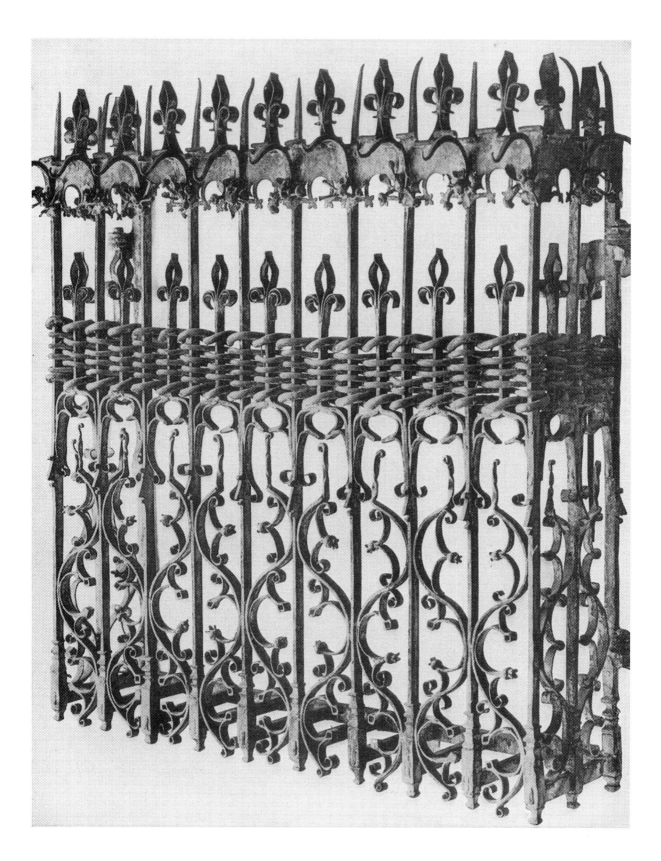

95. Italy, 16th century—Window Grille. Musée Le Secq des Tournelles, Rouen

96. Italy, 16th century—Gates. St. Mark's Church, Rome

97. Italy, 16th century—Fanlight Grilles, Lucca

98. North Italy, 16th century—Doorway Grille

99. North Italy, 16th century—Gate, Trieste Cathedral

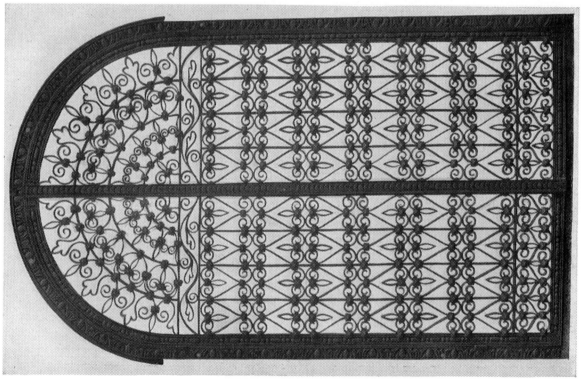

100. North Italy, 16th century—Grilles. Schloss-Museum, Berlin

101. North Italy, end of the 16th century—Grilles. Schloss-Museum, Berlin

102. Germany, 16th century—Gate. Germanic Museum, Nuremberg

103. Germany, 16th century—Above: Fanlight Grille, Nuremberg
Below: Window Grille. Victoria and Albert Museum, London

104. Germany, late 16th century—Skylight Grating and Window Grating

105. Germany, 16th century—Ornamental Railings, Brunswick Cathedral

106. Austria, about 1570—Grille with Door, Ambras Castle

107. Austria, about 1570—Well-head Grille, Grafenegg Castle

108. Germany, end of the 16th century—Screen. Germanic Museum, Nuremberg

109. Germany, about 1580—Screen. Ulrichskirche, Augsburg

110. Germany, about 1580—Screen. Ulrichskirche, Augsburg

111. South Germany, end of the 16th century—Church Screen

112. Austrian Work, 16th century—Door with Iron Mounting, Pressburg

113. Germany, 16th to 17th centuries—Grille with Door, Augsburg

114. Germany, late 16th century—Skylight Grating and Window Grille, Freiberg (Saxony)

115. Germany, end of the 16th century—Window Grille from Zittau (Saxony)

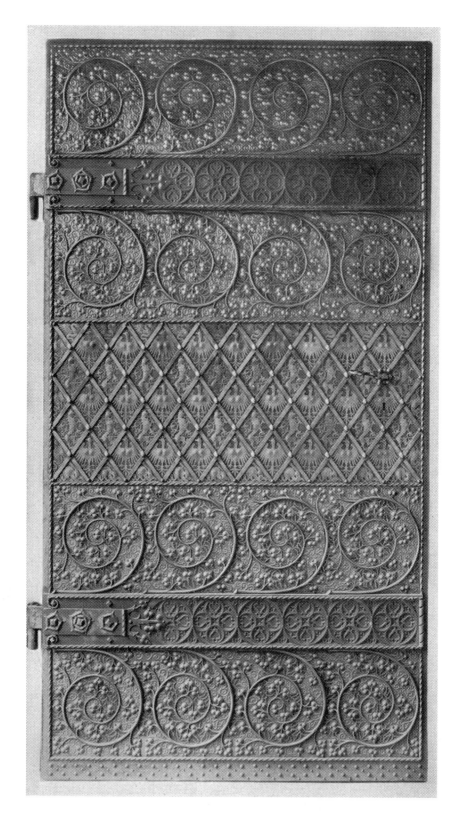

116. Germany, 16th century—Door with Iron Mounting.
Germanic Museum, Nuremberg

117. Door Panels—Above: Germany, middle of the 16th century
Below: Austria, 16th to 17th centuries

118. Germany, 16th to 17th centuries—Door Knockers. Schloss-Museum, Berlin

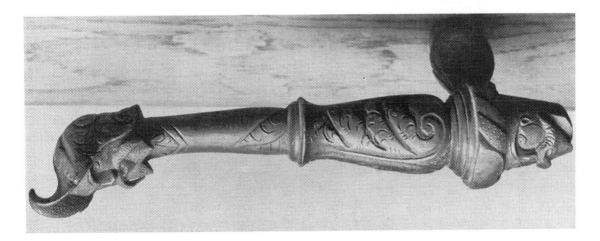

119. Germany, 16th century—Door Knockers and Door Handle. Schloss-Museum, Berlin

120. Germany, 16th century—Door Knockers. Schloss-Museum, Berlin

121. Germany, 16th century—Door Knockers. Schloss-Museum, Berlin

122. Germany, 16th century—Door Knockers. Schloss-Museum, Berlin

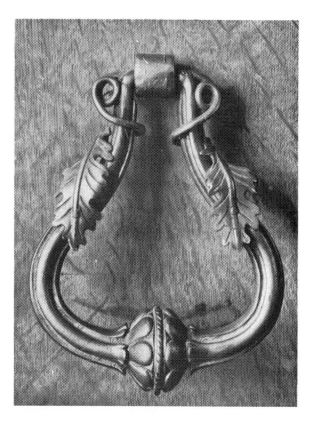

123. Germany, 16th to 17th centuries—Door Knockers. Schloss-Museum, Berlin

124. Germany, about 1595—Screen. The Cathedral, Freiberg (Saxony)

125. Germany, about 1677—Screen. Church of St. Peter, Goerlitz

126. France, 16th century—Gate, Château de Blois

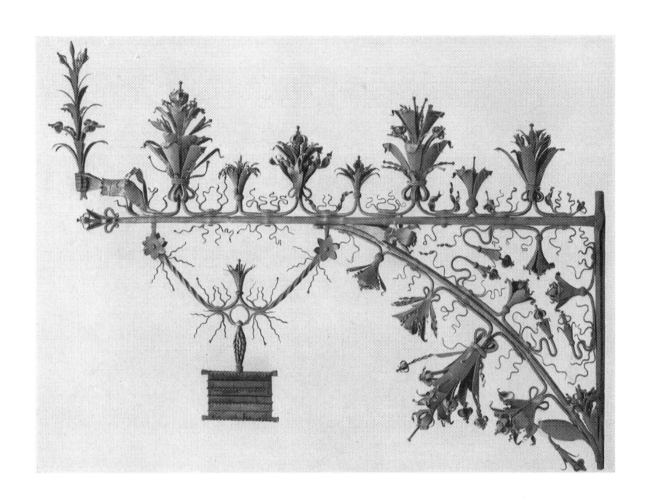

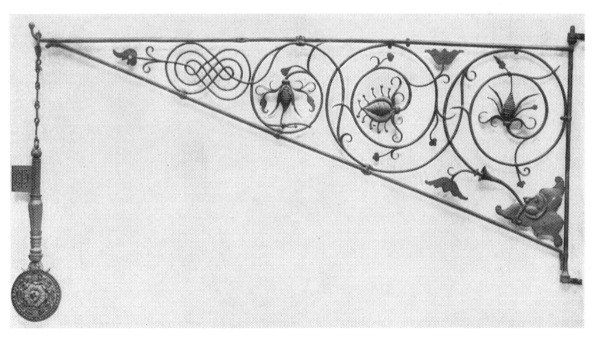

127. Brackets—1) Bruges, early 16th century; 2) Germany, 16th century

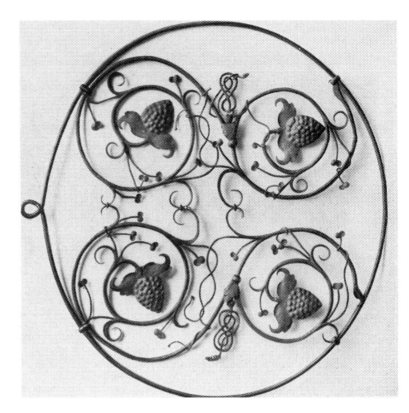

128. Germany, late 16th and early 17th centuries—Grille Cappings and Panels

129. Italy, 17th century—Tabernacle Doors. Left: Schloss-Museum, Berlin
Right: Victoria and Albert Museum, London

130. Germany, late 17th century—Gates, Breslau

131. Germany, 17th century—Gate. Germanic Museum, Nuremberg

132. Germany, late 16th century—Grille

133. France, end of the 16th century—Grille. Musée Carnavalet, Paris

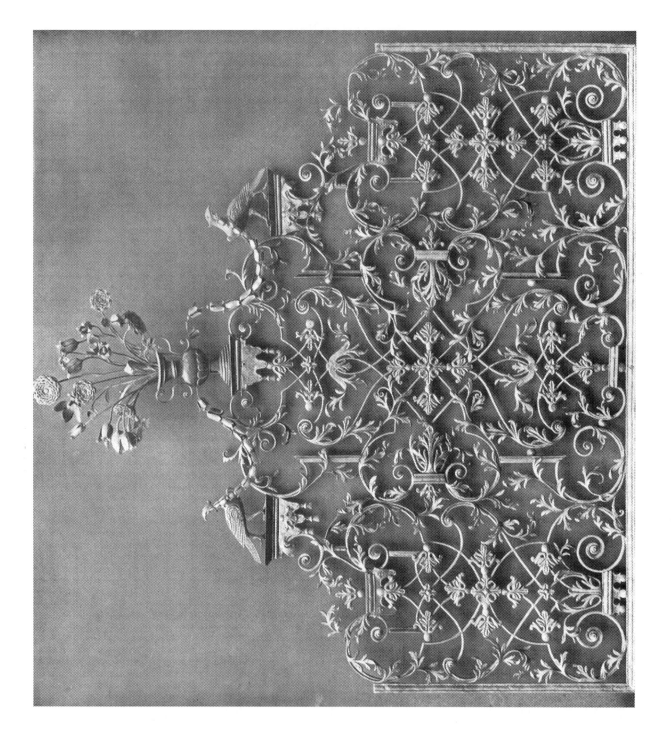

134. Germany, second half of the 17th century—Grille. Dresden

135. Germany, 1637—Grille. Kunstgewerbe Museum, Dresden

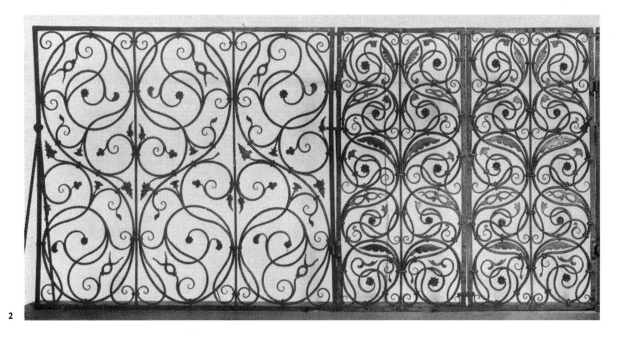

136. South Germany, middle of the 17th century—1) Railings, Munich
2) Part of Railings. Victoria and Albert Museum, London

137. France, 17th century—Grille. Cluny Museum, Paris

138. Denmark, early 17th century—Window Grille, Fredericksborg Castle

139. Denmark, early 17th century—Detail of Chapel Grille. The Cathedral, Röskilde

140. Denmark, 17th century—Chapel Grille. The Cathedral, Röskilde

141. Denmark, 17th century—Grille. Oxholme, Jutland

142. Denmark, about 1650—Chapel Screen. The Cathedral, Ripen

143. Germany, about 1668—Well-head Grille, Neisse (Silesia)

144. Germany, 1630—Fountain Railing, Dantzig

145. Germany, 17th century—1) Railing, Dantzig, about 1620
2) Railings, Goerlitz, late 17th century

146. South Germany, early 17th century—Gates

147. South Germany and North Italy, 17th century—Gates. Schloss-Museum, Berlin

148. South Germany, middle of the 17th century—Window Grilles

149. South Germany, second half of the 17th century—Window Grilles

150. South Germany, first half of the 17th century—Grille Panels from Augsburg and Freiburg

151. South Germany and Hungary, late 17th century—Fanlight Grille and Panel

152. Austria, second half of the 17th century—Screen in the Cathedral, Graz

153. Prague, second half of the 17th century—Screen, Salvatorkirche

154. South Germany, 17th century—Part of a Church Screen

155. Germany, 1700—Grating. St. Mary's Church, Lübeck

156. Prague, middle of the 17th century—Screen, Church of St. George

157. Prague, second half of the 17th century—Grille Panels, Collegium Clementinum

158. Prague, second half of the 17th century—Gates, Collegium Clementinum

159. Prague, second half of the 17th century—Gates, Collegium Clementinum

160. Germany, end of the 17th century
Fanlight Grille from Vienna and Window Grille from Goerlitz

161. North Italy, 17th century—Portions of Grilles

162. Germany, second half of the 17th century—Doors. The Cathedral, Schleswig

163. Germany, second half of the 17th century—Door. The Cathedral, Schleswig

164. Germany, end of the 17th century—Screen. Cathedral, Augsburg

165. Germany, about 1698—Grille with Doors. Ulrichskirche, Augsburg

166. Denmark, about 1700—Centre Panel of the Chapel Screen in the Cathedral, Röskilde

167. Denmark, about 1700—Chapel Screen in the Cathedral, Röskilde

168. Germany, about 1700—Grille. Gewerbe Museum, Nuremberg

169. South Germany, early 18th century—Railing. St. Emeran's Church, Ratisbon

170. Germany, second half of the 17th century—Portions of Grilles
Germanic Museum, Nuremberg

171. Germany, early 18th century—Fanlight Grilles

172. Germany, early 18th century—Grille, from Cologne
Victoria and Albert Museum, London

173. South Germany, about 1726
Part of a Screen Gate in the Old Chapel, Regensburg

174. South Germany, early 17th century—Gravehead Crosses

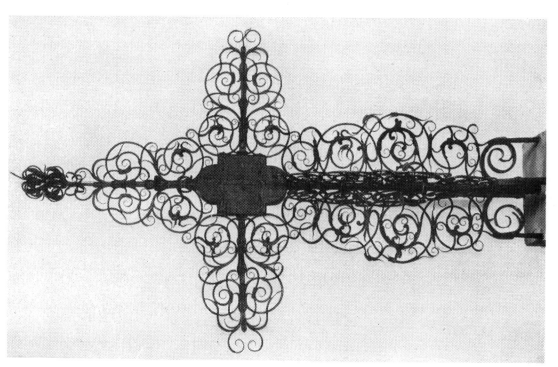

175. South Germany, second half of the 17th century—Gravehead Crosses

176. Italy, 17th century—Above: Fanlight Grille. Schloss-Museum, Berlin
Below: Grille Panel. Victoria and Albert Museum, London

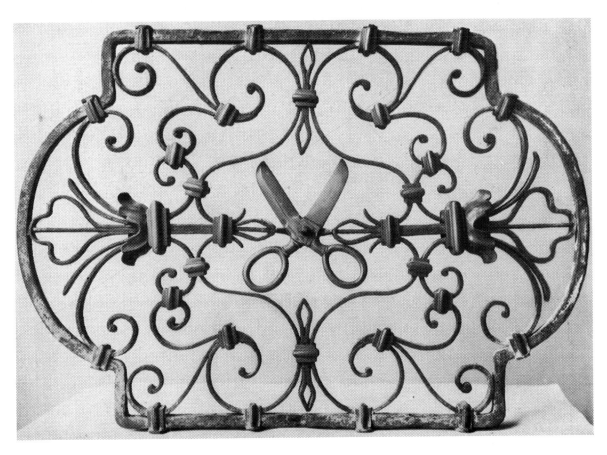

177. Italy, 17th century—Window Grilles. Above: Schloss-Museum, Berlin
Below: Museum of Arts and Crafts, Hamburg

178. North Italy, 17th century—Window Grilles. Left: Victoria and Albert Museum, London. Right: Schloss-Museum, Berlin

179. Italy, 17th century—Screen with Gates. Victoria and Albert Museum, London

180. Italy, 17th century—Grilles. San Giovanni Laterano, Rome

181. France, 17th century—Screen with Gates. Musée Carnavalet, Paris

182. France, about 1661—Screen. Hôtel de Ville, Aix-le-Provence

183. France, 17th century—Railings. 1) Marseilles, Borelli Museum; 2) Versailles Palace

184. France, late 17th century—Grating. Lyons, Couvent de la Visitation

185. France, 17th century—Grille with Gates, Aix

186. France, 17th century—Gate and Railings. Botanical Garden, Angers

187. France, about 1680—Forecourt Screen with Gates, Versailles

188. France, about 1680—Forecourt Screen with Gates (Detail), Versailles

189. France, 17th century—Balustrade. Hôtel Duchâtelet, Paris

190. France, end of the 17th century—Above: Fanlight Grille. Schloss-Museum, Berlin
Below: Window Grille. Musée Le Secq des Tournelles, Rouen

191. France, 17th century—Window Grille. Cluny Museum, Paris

192. France, early 18th century—Banister, Dijon

193. France, early 18th century—1) Balustrade, Dijon
2) Balustrade, Victoria and Albert Museum, London

194. France, 17th century—Balustrade, Fontainebleau

195. France, 17th century—Portions of Balustrade, Fontainebleau

196. France, 17th century—Grille

197. England, about 1700—Railing. Victoria and Albert Museum, London

198. England, about 1700—Screen from Hampton Court. Victoria and Albert Museum, London

199. England, early 18th century—Balustrade. Victoria and Albert Museum, London

200. England, 18th century—Sections of Banisters. Victoria and Albert Museum, London

201. England, early 18th century—Railings. Victoria and Albert Museum, London

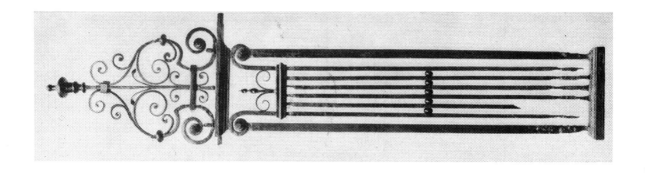

202. England, early 18th century—Bracket and Pilaster. Victoria and Albert Museum, London

203. England, early 18th century—Brackets and Ornamental Top of Railings. Victoria and Albert Museum, London

204. England, early 18th century—Gateway. Victoria and Albert Museum, London

205. England, 18th century—Part of Railings. Victoria and Albert Museum, London

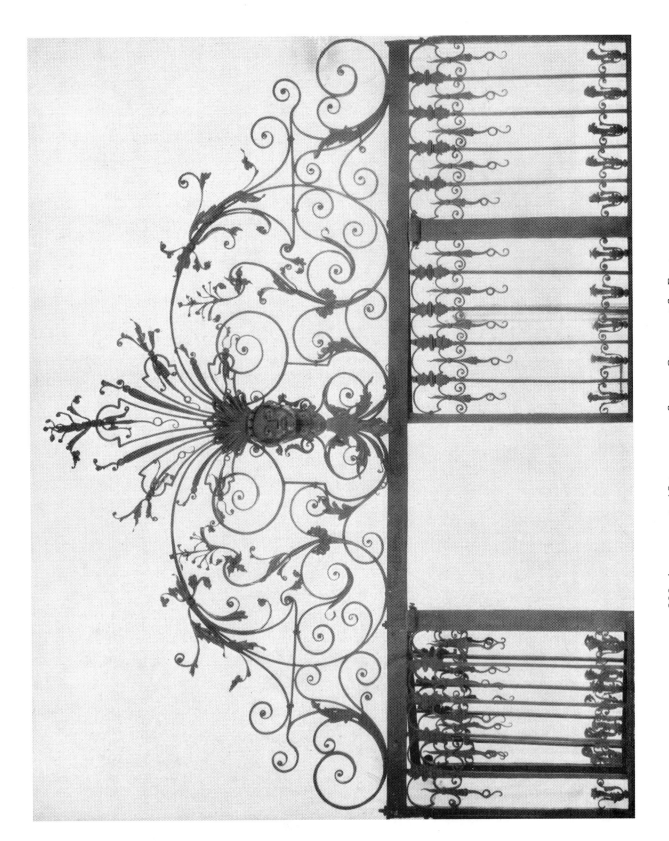

206. Austria, early 18th century—Screen, Chapter of St. Florian

207. Italy, early 18th century—Grille from Venice. Schloss-Museum, Berlin

208. Italy, early 18th century—Fanlight Grille and Gate

209. Italy, early 18th century—Gates and Grille Panel
Victoria and Albert Museum, London

210. North Italy, early 18th century—Gates. Schloss-Museum, Berlin

211. France, early 18th century—1) Balustrade, Lyons; 2) Grille. Musée Carnavalet, Paris

212. France, first half of the 18th century—Banister, Aix-en-Provence

213. France, early 18th century—Banister, Aix-en-Provence

214. France, 18th century—Section of Banister, Aix-en-Provence

215. Alsatia, first half of the 18th century—Sign Boards

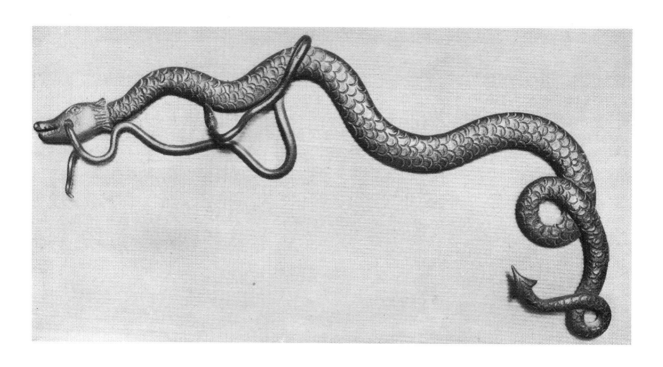

216. France, early 18th century—Brackets

217. South Germany, early 18th century—1) Ornamental Top of Counter; 2) Part of Railings

218. Germany, about 1700—Portions of a Grille from Augsburg

219. Prague, early 18th century—Railings in the Cathedral

220. Prague, early 18th century—Gates, Strachow Church

221. Prague, early 18th century—Gates, Strachow Church

222. Austria, early 18th century—Grille. Monastery Church, Stans

223. Austria, early 18th century—Window Screen, Steyr

224. Austria, early 18th century—Gates. Cathedral, Gratz

225. Austria, early 18th century—Section of Gates. Cathedral, Gratz

226. Germany, 18th century—Screen. St. Cross Church, Augsburg

227. Germany, about 1712—Screen. St. Ulric's Church, Augsburg

228. Germany, about 1712—Screen. St. Ulric's Church, Augsburg

229. Germany, early 18th century—Screen. Cathedral, Constance

230. France and South Germany, early 18th century—Skylight Gratings

231. Brunn (Moravia), early 18th century—Ornamental Railings. Church of the Minorities

232. Austria, early 18th century—Grille Panel. Collegiate Church, Dürnstein

233. Austria, early 18th century—Screen. Minster, Dürnstein

234. Prague, early 18th century—Grille. Strachowkirche

235. Austria, about 1720—Gates. Belvedere Palace, Vienna

236. Austria, about 1720—Gates. Belvedere Palace, Vienna

237. Austria, about 1720—Gates. Belvedere Palace, Vienna

238. Germany, first half of the 18th century—Skylight Grating and Window Parapet

239. Germany, about 1740—Gates. Town Hall, Frankfort

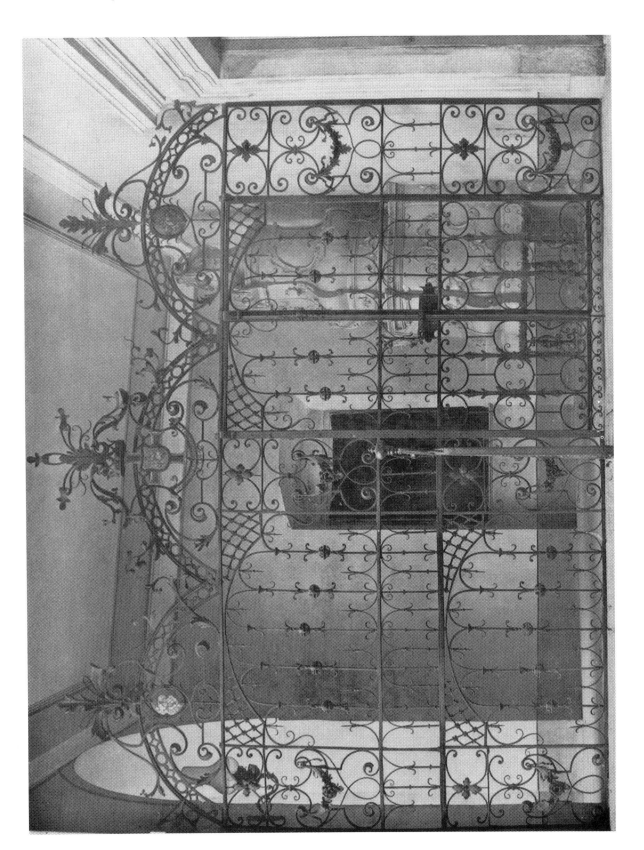

240. Tirol, about 1744—Grille. Deutschordenshaus, Bozen

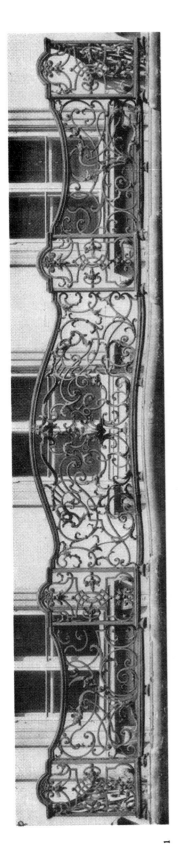

241. Germany, middle of the 18th century—1) Balustrade, Hanover; 2) Balustrade. Palace Church, Ellingen

1

2

242. Germany, early 18th century—Section of Gates

243. Germany, 18th century—Chapel Screen, Hirschberg

244. Prague, early 18th century—Door with Iron Mounting, St. Thomas' Church

245. 1) Vienna, about 1744—Section of Screen, St. John's Chapel
2) Zürich, about 1726—Skylight Grating

246. Prague, early 18th century—Door Handle and Knocker, Clam-Gallas Palace

247. 1) France, early 18th century—Knocker; 2) Germany, 17th–18th century—Door Knobs

248. France, 18th century—Knockers, Bordeaux

249. France, 18th century—Knockers, Bordeaux

250. Germany, early 18th century—Knocker. Germanic Museum, Nuremberg

251. South Germany, first half of the 18th century—Mountings of Wrought Iron

252. Germany, about 1724—Ornaments in Wrought Iron

253. South Germany, middle of the 18th century—Top Part of Grave Cross

254. Austria, about 1720—Window Screen, Vienna

255. South Germany, early 18th century—1) Skylight Grating; 2) Fireguard

256. Prague, middle of the 18th century—Gates

257. South Germany, middle of the 18th century—Skylight Gratings

258. Germany, early 18th century—Brackets

259. South Germany, middle of the 18th century—Sign Brackets

260. Switzerland, early 18th century—Gates, Bâle

261. Switzerland, 18th century—Railings, Bâle

262. France, early 18th century—Palace Gates, Dampierre (Aube)

265. France, 18th century—Skylight Gratings, Lyons

266. France, about 1730—Gates. Archbishop's Palace, Sens

267. France, middle of the 18th century—Cathedral Screen, Nancy

268. France, middle of the 18th century—Gateway. Stanislas Square, Nancy

269. France, middle of the 18th century—Gateway. Stanislas Square by Jean Lamour, Nancy

270. France, middle of the 18th century—Part of Gateway. Stanislas Square, Nancy

271. France, middle of the 18th century—Part of Railings. Stanislas Square, Nancy

272. France, middle of the 18th century—Gates. Cathedral, Lyons

273. France, middle of the 18th century—Gates. Cathedral, Lyons

274. France, middle of the 18th century—Balustrade, Lyons

275. Lyons and Zürich, middle of the 18th century—Balustrade

276. Germany, about 1743—Balustrade Panels. Brühl Castle (Rhine)

277. Germany, about 1743—Lantern and Banisters. Brühl Palace (Rhine)

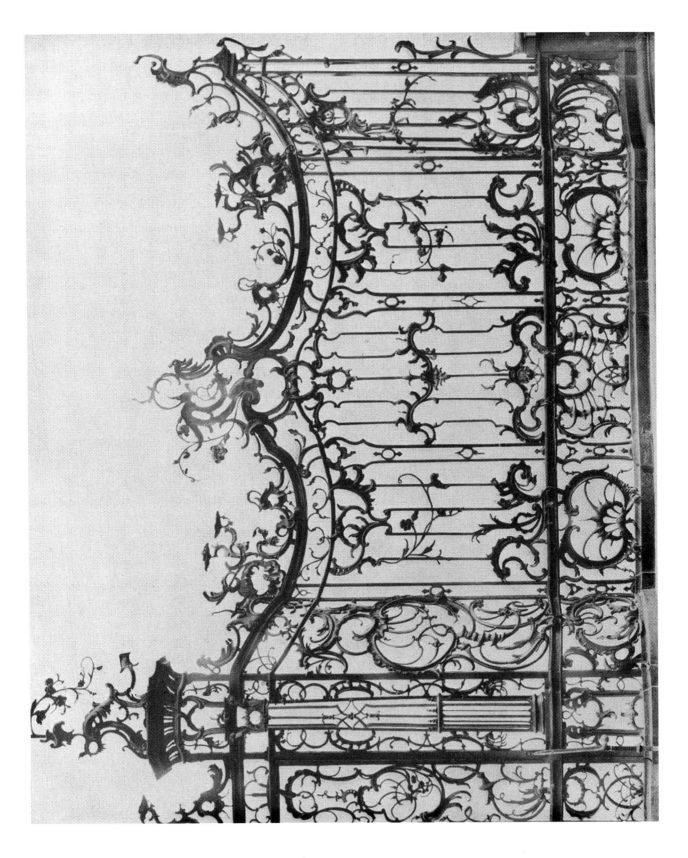

278. Germany, about 1750—Railings, Würzburg

279. Vienna, first half of the 18th century—Screen. Church of the Dominicans

280. Austria, first half of the 18th century—Screen. Church of the Franciscans, Salzburg

281. Austria, first half of the 18th century—Gates. Church of the Franciscans, Salzburg

282. Hungary, middle of the 18th century—Details of Wrought Iron Work, Pressburg

283. Germany, about 1725—Details of Wrought Iron Work. National Museum, Munich

284. Hungary, middle of the 18th century—Folding Door, Wrought Iron

285. Austria, middle of the 18th century—Gates, Reichenberg Chapter

286. Austria, first half of the 18th century—Gates. Church of St. Peter, Salzburg

287. Germany, middle of the 18th century—Garden Gates, Nuremberg

288. Germany, about 1750—Section of Gates, Würzburg Palace

289. Germany, about 1750—Section of Gates, Würzburg Castle

290. Germany, about 1750—Section of Ornamental Railings, Würzburg Castle

291. Germany, about 1750—Section of Ornamental Railings, Würzburg Castle

292. Germany, about 1750—Gates, Würzburg Castle

293. Germany, about 1750—Gates, Würzburg Castle

294. Hungary, middle of the 18th century—Gates, Heves

295. Germany, middle of the 18th century—Gates, Roggenburg Church

296. South Germany, middle of the 18th century—Gates

297. South Germany, middle of the 18th century—Gates

298. Switzerland, middle of the 18th century—Gates, Zürich

299. Switzerland, 18th century—Gates. Bâle, Rittergasse

300. Switzerland, middle of the 18th century—Window Grilles, Bâle

301. Germany and Switzerland, second half of 18th century—Window Grilles. 1) Rothenburg; 2) Bâle

302. Switzerland, middle of the 18th century—Choir Railings, St. Gallen Minster

303. South Germany, about 1760—Screen, Ober-Marchtal Church

304. Germany, 1720–1750—1) Bracket; 2) Ornamental Top of Railings; 3) Grave Cross

305. South Germany and Switzerland, first half of the 18th century—Skylight Gratings

306. Italy, early 18th century—Part of Church Barrier, Bologna.

307. France, second half of the 18th century—Part of Church Barrier. St. Germain l'Auxerrois, Paris

308. France, second half of the 18th century—Banister. Versailles, Grand Trianon

309. France, second half of the 18th century—Banister, Compiègne Castle

310. France, second half of the 18th century—Banister, Paris Admiralty

311. 1) Austria, Fanlight Grille; 2) France, Banister, Dijon—both 2nd half of 18th century

312. France, second half of the 18th century—Gates. École Militaire, Paris

313. France, second half of the 18th century—Gates. Palais de Justice, Paris

314. Germany, second half of the 18th century—Railings. Veitshöchheim Castle

315. Germany, second half of the 18th century—Ornamental Top of Railings. Veitshöchheim Castle

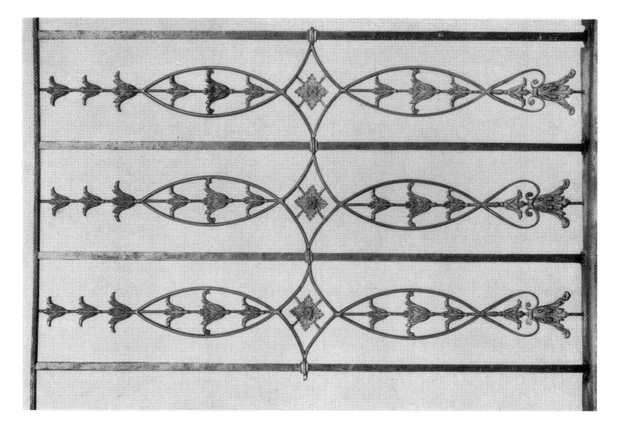

316. 1) Austria, Window Grille; 2) England, Part of Railing—both 2nd half of 18th century

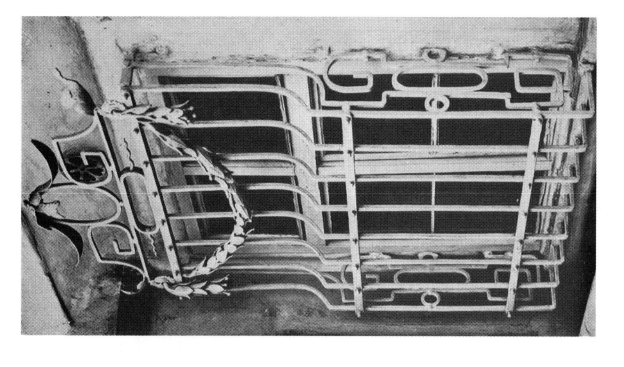

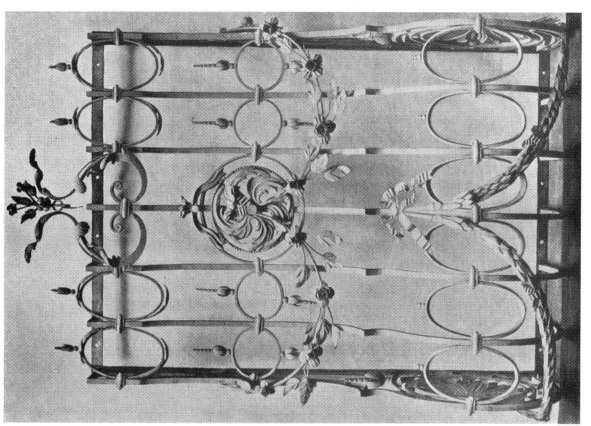

317. Austria and South Germany, second half of 18th century—Window Grilles

318. Germany, 18th century—Lantern and Chandelier

319. Germany, second half of the 18th century—Wrought Iron Lanterns

320. Germany, second half of the 18th century—1) and 3) Fanlight Grilles
2) Ornamental Top of Counter